Living with Deaf-Blindness
nine profiles

developed and written by
Carol Yoken
Technical Service Specialist
The National Academy
of Gallaudet College

published by
The National Academy
of Gallaudet College

Gallaudet College is an equal opportunity employer/ educational institution. Programs and services of Gallaudet College receive substantial financial support from the Department of Health, Education, and Welfare.

ISBN # 0-934336-01-6 paper back edition
ISBN # 0-934336-00-8 hard back edition

Library of Congress Catalog Card # 79-52740
Copyright 1979 by Gallaudet College, Washington, D.C.

Foreword

Traditionally, students preparing to enter one of the helping professions undertake internships with the particular populations they plan to serve. For those interested in a career working with deaf-blind persons, or interested in learning more about this disability group, the goal of getting to know the population appears unattainable due to obvious obstacles of communication. It is essentially for that reason that this book has been prepared.

Obtaining reliable information about the experiences, problems, and capabilities of any group that one wishes to work with is basic to career preparation. Some works are available by experienced and competent professionals who describe from their perspective the problems and needs of deaf-blind people. Other books–biographies and autobiographies of exceptional deaf-blind persons–also offer some insight into problems deaf-blind people encounter. In developing this book we have attempted to provide a forum for a varied group of individuals to describe the circumstances of their lives. The result, we hope, allows students to make their own interpretations, form their own conclusions, and develop their own conceptions of what living as a deaf-blind individual may mean.

Gallaudet College has a long history of service to deaf people. In addition, a small but not insignificant number of its students and former students live and have lived with deaf-blindness. The College is committed to encouraging the development of effective services for deaf-blind citizens and will continue to pursue opportunities whereby its resources can be used to meet that objective.

Albert T. Pimentel, Director
The National Academy of Gallaudet College

Acknowledgments

Rehabilitation workers throughout the country coordinated the interviews and cooperated in myriad other ways. Although their names are omitted here to maintain confidentiality, they have our deep appreciation. We are also grateful to the professionals in related fields who read and criticized the manuscript:

Mary Flynn, M.S.W., National Catholic School of Social Service, Catholic University

Robert Mehan, Ed.D., Department of Counseling, Gallaudet College

Luther Robinson, M.D., St. Elizabeths Hospital, National Institute of Mental Health

McCay Vernon, Ph.D., Department of Psychology, Western Maryland College.

And to the deaf-blind people who allowed themselves to be interviewed and written about, we offer our sincere and abundant thanks.

Carol Yoken
Technical Service Specialist
The National Academy of Gallaudet College

Contents

Introduction	1
Profiles:	
Randy Cooper	7
Bill Moore	25
Lucian Cordaro	41
Joan Tiller	61
Ross Adams	79
Mike Price	91
Hanna Berzinsh	105
Mary Barker Boyd	123
Wilbur Martinson	139
Conclusion	157
Appendixes	161

Introduction

SERVICES TO DEAF-BLIND PEOPLE

Deaf-blindness is a unique disability. The sensory deprivation is almost unimaginable to the normally hearing-sighted individual, as well as to the person who is either deaf or blind. Some consequences of that deprivation are obvious—limitations of communication and mobility. The scope of the limitations and their psychological implications, however, may be more far-reaching than those who are not deaf-blind realize. Indeed, we know little of the normal feelings and normal development of the person who lives the abnormal circumstance of being both deaf and blind.

Despite the fame of Laura Bridgman and Helen Keller, the plight of deaf-blind people in this country has been ill-addressed. The Federal Government estimates 21,000 deaf-blind children and adults in the United States. Yet they constitute a largely invisible minority. Rarely do they participate in social or cultural activities in their communities or receive even minimal social services to aid daily living. Rarely are they offered effective education and rehabilitation programs.

The picture is not entirely bleak. Important commitments have been made during the 1960's and 1970's to establish and expand services. The Industrial Home for the Blind (IHB) in Brooklyn, New York, under an agreement with the U.S. Department of Health, Education, and Welfare (HEW) established the Helen Keller National Center for Deaf-Blind

Youths and Adults in Sands Point, New York. The National Center continues and enlarges the work of the IHB's Anne Macy Sullivan Service, which for years had been one of few programs in the country providing rehabilitation for deaf-blind people. Deaf-blind men and women 18 years and older can participate in the National Center's residential program or find services in their home states from agencies affiliated with the Center. The ten Regional Centers for Services to Deaf-Blind Children, administered by the Bureau of Education for the Handicapped, HEW, provide wide-ranging services for deaf-blind children and youth through the age of 21. Gallaudet College provides support services to deaf-blind students in its undergraduate and graduate degree programs, and sponsors evening courses for deaf-blind adults and a summer learning vacation program for families with a deaf-blind child. It develops materials for professional workers and provides nationwide advocacy and consultation services for agencies and families of deaf-blind individuals. The San Francisco Lighthouse for the Blind has been a pioneer in using peer counseling as well as more traditional training to develop vocational and independent living skills in deaf-blind adults. Various other agencies, including many state vocational rehabilitation offices, have initiated services for deaf-blind clients through their programs serving deaf individuals or blind individuals.

Despite the important progress these programs represent, we have barely scratched the surface. A primary shortcoming of rehabilitation services for deaf-blind people is the lack of specific training for the counselor or social worker entering the field. Frequently those who become "deaf-blind specialists," or who are assigned one or two deaf-blind clients, have been counselors for blind persons. Although experienced in work with the blind, they are not trained for even rudimentary communication with the many deaf-blind individuals using American Sign Language. Nor are they informed of the life problems that may confront deaf-blind individuals–whether totally or partially impaired, in the early stages of adjustment to a sudden loss, undergoing a progressive loss, or living daily with a stable condition. Unaware of the kinds of circumstances deaf-blind people face, new counselors are equally unprepared for their own work, for the experiences of the deaf-blind individual frequently translate into emotional concerns, and as such can make or break a program of rehabilitation.

THE DEVELOPMENT OF THIS BOOK

The purpose of this book is to introduce students and professional workers to issues in the lives of deaf-blind individuals. The nine people whose stories are included here constitute a deliberately varied group. Four individuals were born with severe or profound hearing losses and gradually lost most or all of their vision from *retinitis pigmentosa*. Two suffered sudden, concurrent, and nearly total losses, one as a teenager, from illness or surgery; the other in his 20's from a motorcycle accident. Two people had severely impaired vision as young children, recovered some sight, then developed hearing losses. Another individual lost most of his vision in his early 20's from glaucoma, then 20 years later, most of his hearing in Meniere's Syndrome. These individuals differ also in characteristics apart from the disabilities. They range in age from 23 to 71; in education, from completing only the sixth grade to earning a doctorate. One person has never worked outside of the home; others have been employed in sheltered workshops, for public agencies, and in private industry. They have different family backgrounds and live in various regions of the United States and in communities of various sizes.

No absolute measurements of hearing impairment and vision impairment delimit the population of deaf-blind individuals, although a standard description of deaf-blindness used by agencies is legal blindness and severe to profound hearing loss. Legal blindness is defined as the inability, with the best corrective lenses, to see at a distance of 20 feet any more than someone with normal vision can see at a distance of 200 feet, or peripheral vision limited to 20 degrees or less (tunnel vision). Hearing impairment is more difficult to quantify and categorize. A hearing loss can be classified as mild, moderate, severe, or profound, depending on the intensity (or loudness) a sound must be for a person to hear it. Sound frequency, however, also affects ability to hear, and a person who can hear low-pitched sounds at a given loudness may not be able to hear higher-pitched sounds at an equal volume. These variations are important in assessing an individual's hearing, for speech sounds differ in pitch. One who cannot hear all parts of a word often cannot understand speech. Deafness, as opposed to lesser hearing loss, is most often described as the inability to hear and understand speech.

Functional considerations help clarify who is considered deaf-blind. Because deaf-blindness is a dual disability, with the effects of one loss compounding those of the other, it is usefully described as losses of vision and hearing that together make methods of communication, and therefore programs of all kinds, that are suitable for the deaf or blind person inadequate for the affected person. Although some individuals in the book can hear or see under certain conditions of lighting, amplification, proximity, or quietness, none can adequately receive communication in a majority of everyday situations without special assistance. Among those in the book, all but one person (who is not legally blind) fall into the standard, accepted description of deaf-blindness.

The project to prepare this collection began in January 1978. The National Academy of Gallaudet College (formerly Public Service Programs) sent letters to state agencies for the blind and other organizations inviting cooperation. Initial agency participation involved contacting deaf-blind persons, explaining the purpose and methods of the project, and, with an individual's consent, forwarding brief biographical information to the College.

Several months later the process of interviewing began. Carol Yoken of Gallaudet College, interviewer and writer for the project, travelled to individuals' home communities, interviewing each deaf-blind person and, with the person's permission, relatives, agency workers, and members of the local community. When permission was granted, agency records were reviewed.

Methods of interviewing were modified to suit the needs and preferences of each deaf-blind person. Ms. Yoken questioned by writing on paper, speaking loudly, printing on the palm or shoulder, fingerspelling or signing within the individual's visual field or in his hands. Deaf-blind individuals responded by speaking, signing, fingerspelling, writing, typing, and combinations of these methods. Sign language interpreters were used—once for all interviews with an individual, and in other cases briefly to check the accuracy of Ms. Yoken's comprehension of signs. The differences in modes of communication, as well as differences in individuals' personalities and backgrounds, were reflected in the amount of time used in a set of interviews. Interviews with an individual lasted from several days to a full week. The shortest set of interviews required less than 12 hours; the longest, almost 40 hours. A tape recorder was used, again with each person's permission. Deaf-blind people with recordable speech were recorded directly. Otherwise, Ms. Yoken (or the interpreter) spoke into the machine.

Questionnaires were developed before starting the interviews. They outlined topics fundamental to the project's purpose—an individual's early family life, schooling, work experiences, and social activities. Although the questions were of limited value in eliciting information, they were retained as a frame of reference for basic topics. At the same time, despite the regularity with which certain issues appeared, each interview with a different deaf-blind person was conducted without presumptions of what would be important to him or her. (See Appendix A for the interview questions.)

Before beginning a set of interviews, each deaf-blind individual signed an authorization for the interview and publication of the subsequent profile. Each person had the opportunity to read a final version of the story (or otherwise have it communicated) and have changes made when the information presented as factual was incorrect. The more nebulous impressions of the interviewer/writer would not necessarily be changed. Individuals were presented the option, both when signing the authorization, and later, after reading the finished profile, of having a pseudonym used and other identifying information disguised. In some cases, when permission was granted, Gallaudet College made the decision to employ pseudonyms or alter other information to preserve the privacy of the individual's family or associates. (See Appendix B for copies of the authorization statements.)

Criteria for selection of interviewees were established at the outset of the project. Initial criteria were to include individuals of various ages and with various causes of deaf-blindness. Two restrictions were adopted: to interview only adults and only those with sufficient communication skills to relate their experiences. These criteria reflect the primary purpose of the book–to have individuals tell their own stories from which readers can draw meaningful conclusions.

Certain omissions from the book were unintentional. There is limited ethnic and racial diversity among those written about, and no women raising children are included. Those limitations reflect, in part, that working through vocational rehabilitation to select individuals, we had a largely, though not entirely, homogenous sample of white men. Interviews were conducted with several deaf-blind mothers, but they did not result in new information for actual profiles.

The profiles presented here reflect information provided by the deaf-blind individuals, their families and acquaintances, records, and the impressions of the interviewer/writer. When conflicting information was obtained from various sources, attempts were made to clarify understanding with the deaf-blind person. When more than one version of an event or relationship remained, the different viewpoints are presented. The profiles should be considered accounts of individuals' experiences and feelings, based primarily on information relayed by the individuals in brief meetings at particular points in life. Any errors or misconceptions in the stories reflect limitations inherent when the interviewer, an outsider, prepares the profiles. It is hoped the book will encourage others to undertake similar investigations based on firsthand information from deaf-blind individuals and that such future work will enhance our understanding of living with deaf-blindness.

Randy Cooper*

"You wanna know who my true love is? Loretta Lynn. I love her, I do. 'Yes, I'm proud to be a coal miner's daughter.' I've told Cathy so it's no secret: when she gets up on the stage and tells the people she'd like to dedicate this song to me, Cathy gotta go. Oh yeah. Loretta Lynn. Anne Murray. Ray Price and "For the Goodtimes." You don't know 'em? You can forget about me goin' to Washington. I want to stay right here with this good ol' country music." Randy shook his head before he spoke again. Is it resignation or mock resignation? "But to tell you the truth, since I lost my hearin', I lost a little a my affection for Loretta Lynn."

Clearwater, Tennessee is a town about 20 miles from the city of Memphis, in the northern part of the state near the Arkansas border. After the highway, the long roads out to Randy Cooper's house span fields of low-lying crops–soybeans, cotton, okra–and tall stalks of corn. Shielding the crops from the road are wild plants–green reeds, wheat-colored Johnson's grass, soft Queen Anne's Lace, and occasional patches of tiny white daisies. Randy lives on Webster Road, Route One, Clearwater, with his wife, Cathy, who is 27 and their daughters Pumpkin (Lisa) and Laurie, 3 years old and 14 months old, respectively. Randy is 30. He has been deaf and nearly blind for 5 years. I don't know what he would say after reading my description of him. Coming from

---

*Names of people and places have been changed, including cities, towns, states, state prisons, and the state school.

me, both a city person ("Oh yeah, I forgot you're from Washington.") and someone he knows likes him immensely, he'd probably fall back in his chair and laugh. To me, he looks like a combination of a hillbilly and a redneck. His hair is combed up from his forehead, but it is long and airy and falls back down. He is big and a bit flabby, and he has a "gut" that he explains ruefully is the product of milk and soft drinks. Five years ago when he was living on beer, his drinking never showed. He wears jeans and a shirt three-quarters of the way unbuttoned. The cut off sleeves reveal two or three fading tatoos on each arm.

"My life story. I was born here in Mills County. We lived in Mackey for awhile; Dad farmed down there. Well, I had a brother, T.J. He got run over gettin' off a school bus and Dad just had to get away, so he bought this place up here. We moved when I was 3. We farmed this place. He built this house for us, and, uh, well, I've lived, you might say, most of my life here. I got married (his first marriage); I worked hanging sheetrock in Alabama; worked at General Motors Company, Illinois. My younger sister, next to me, married an Air Force guy. They're in Phoenix, Arizona. Then I've got two other sisters. One lives in town and the other lives up the road here about 4 or 5 miles. My mom is living. She lives, I call it, across the garden."

Randy hemmed and hawed at this point and was uncomfortable about breaking into the subsequent story of his life. I learned later his hesitance was not from embarrassment or shame so much as from his not wanting to ruin this book.

"All right. I'll tell you about my life. I done the time for what I done and got caught at. I ain't gonna tell you nothin' I done and didn't get caught." Randy laughed at this and at many of his remarks and anecdotes throughout the interviews. So did I. "I haven't had a life like most people. My life, from 15 to 25, I was an outlaw. When I was 13, I started messin' up, more or less. Got caught breakin' into a store. I got probation. I was still in school, layin' out and wantin' to quit. Well, I wasn't 15 when I did quit. They sent me to a boy's school–reformatory, you know–in Nashville. I run off. My mom and dad talked me into goin' back. I went back and stayed a week, then run off again. I stayed home 8 months."

Randy's father died about that time and he started getting into more serious trouble. "I wouldn't work. I hung around all the time and, uh, well, I got married when I was 17. (His wife was 15; they had two daughters.) And that didn't help me either, as far as straightenin' up; I still wasn't growed up. They got me for two cars-stealin' 'em and strippin' 'em-and the judge declared me 'incorrigible.' Well, them cases went along in court for a year or two and they caught me for another car. When they tried me for that, they brought up the other ones, too. Give me 2 years. While I was in, my wife divorced me."

"I did 16 months on 2 years and got out. Stayed out a year, then they busted me for a burglary. Breakin' and enterin'. I got out on bond and went up north and got me a car. What it was, I was stayin' in a trailer park and this guy I know come by one night and we were drinkin' and he kept sayin', 'Boy, sure would like to go to Tennessee.' He said that three or four times-he sure would like to go to Tennessee-so I just told him I'd be back in a minute. I stepped down a coupl'a trailers and 'borrowed' a car. Wheeled back up in front of the trailer and said, 'Let's go.' He changed his mind, so I came to Tennessee myself. Week or so later, they caught me with the car and a sawed-off shotgun. When they locked me up, I didn't get out before I got to 3 years on the breakin' and enterin'.

"I went off to Jackson Prison in Tennessee and they brought me back after 6 months. I was doin' state time. This car and shotgun was federal. They didn't try me for the shotgun, but they gave me 4 years for the car and runnin' interstate, and I went back to Jackson. Stayed there 9 or 10 months more; they were gonna tear it down, so they transferred us to a new prison in farther south Tennessee. I stayed about 6 months and I made it to parole to the federal. I left Hudson and went to Tallahassee, Florida, federal. I had trouble down there with Blacks and they transferred me to Terre Haute, Indiana. Tallahassee is more or less a kid's prison, young boys. Indiana-more criminal men or somethin'. I stayed there 3½ years 'til I was 25, 1972. Stayed out almost a year. Got out May 1st, 1972 and May the 12th, 1973, I hit that fence post. I was on a motorcycle and it went off the road.

"There was somethin' in me those 10 years that made me want to do somethin', try to outsmart the other man, I guess. I don't know where my life came in, I mean the way I lived. It sure wasn't the way I was raised. I just got on the wrong road or somethin'. It was in me, though. Knowin' if I got caught, I'd have to pay. Was I happy? I don't know. I thought I was happy, anyway. I did as I pleased. I did what I wanted to do.

"In '68, I worked 2 or 3 months in Birmingham, hangin' sheetrock, me and a coupl'a my cousins. We might'a worked 2 or 3 days, hangin' rock. We could be workin, makin' that money, hangin' them boards. Some crazy thing would mention goin' fishin.' Get the tools, loaded up. Went down there in '68. We rented a house, had a yard. We got us a croquet set. We could be on the job workin'. Somebody'd mention croquet. In the middle of the day, we'd load up the tools, go home and play croquet. It was livin', I mean. We did as we pleased. But hey, we made good money—a hundred-and-a-half a week and I can't remember when we worked a full week."

During the periods when he was not in prison, Randy would often, on the spur of the moment, in cars that he "borrowed without permission," drive up to see his cousin Kevin in Ludlow, Illinois. He sometimes worked there for a week or two, in a steel mill, a shoe factory, or for General Motors, but the real attraction was the horse races. About his sporadic trips, he says, "From the time I was 17, I was just there and gone, there and gone. The longest I've stayed any place since I was 15 was in prison. Since I hit that fence post I haven't been goin' places. Been livin' here for 3 years now. But until the accident, I couldn't be still. Here, there, Illinois, Alabama. I could go to Mom's and stay anytime I wanted to, but I really had no home, I mean me. I never was around long enough to have a place."

I asked Randy if he had felt confined in prison. "Well, in quarantine. In quarantine you're locked up in a cell 'til they classify you and do odds and ends. But once I was let out in the population, I didn't feel confined. I could move, go to the yard, move around, you know. You're not confined to one cell. Well, at Hancock, I did 7 days in the doghouse one December. I lost 14 pounds. They give you two biscuits for breakfast, a piece of cornbread for dinner, all the water you can drink for supper. You have a pair of coveralls on a concrete floor. Got a bucket for a bathroom. Every 3 days, though, you get a complete meal. You can hold it in your hands (laugh)."

"The first time I went up, I thought I wanted to come home for Christmas. So me and about eight others jumped over the fence. They caught us comin' down the road and I told myself, 'You got this time to do and that's the only way you're gonna get out.'

"But there's a lot goin' on in a prison. Home brew. One time we scored some sugar and yeast to make us some home brew. We done made ourselves about 5 gallons, boy, mmm. I gotta go round on the other side of the tier to see somebody, and there's this guard in the cubicle who opens doors and things for men, but I'm out, I'm honorable. I cut around there with a cup full of julep. I get to the door and he hollers for me, 'C'mere.' I got the cup in my hand. I step right back down the hall and into the cell, drink it quick. I go up and see what he wants. He looks at me, says, 'Cooper, you have some more julep, you don't offer me a drink, I'm gonna lock you up.' 'Yes sir, boss man.' Let me go.

"I got some of these tattoos put on in prison one time when we had a little julep. Used to have one that said, 'Six feet of walking hell.' There was a cop asked me, 'That gets you in a lot of fights, don't it?' I told him, 'Nothin' I can't walk away from.' It's off now, burned 'em off in '69 in jail.

"I've seen a lot of men killed in prison. That bothered me sometimes. Senseless killings, no reason. They were just kids. There was this boy and another boy owed him 50 cents, and he didn't have it. Well, this boy who had the 50 cents owed to him, he killed this boy. Then he walked up and told the warden, 'I got up this mornin' . . . if anybody made me mad, I'd kill him.' And he killed this boy for 50 cents. In prison there's knives–homemade knives. If you need one, you can get one. I got into it with a guy in quarantine once. At Jackson. And Charles Hutchins, I know'd him before. He was there before me and already in population. He came in from work that day and heard about me havin' trouble. You could come on the second floor and holler up a screen to the third floor, to quarantine. Hey, he was right there, soon as he heard about it, askin' me did I want a knife. Friends . . . ."

After his release from prison in 1972, Randy decided to straighten up. He went home and started hanging sheetrock in Memphis. He went to Ludlow for a few weeks to earn more money, then came home for a weekend and spent all of his cash. (He once made $1,700 one Monday morning from a stick-up. The next Monday he was broke, he says, "and didn't have a thing to show for what I spent that $1,700 on. Just a lot of miles, state to state, ridin' here and there, drinkin'.") He went to his sister and asked for $16 to drive back to Illinois, but she refused to loan it. "To show you the kind of person I was, I went out, got in my car, and told myself, 'Cooper, you will get that money.' I didn't go back to work. I started outlawin' again. I could have drove 20 miles and asked Mom for the money. Not me. I started stealin'."

In April of 1973, he met Cathy in Clearwater. They knew each other for a month, then went to Alabama for a few days. They came back and got married. Two weeks later, Randy was supposed to ride down to Alabama with a cousin and pick up the things he and Cathy had left there. He does not remember anything about the day. But he was riding on a motorcycle, it hit a fence post, and he suffered a severe basal skull fracture, a linear fracture on the right side of his skull, facial lacerations, multiple abrasions, pupillary changes in his eyes, and fluid loss from his ears. The rest of the medical report, describing bleeding, vomiting, and tissue detachment is, despite its clinical terminology, enough to make a reader retch.

He was in the hospital in Memphis for a month, in a coma, before Cathy asked Mrs. Cooper's permission to take him to her mother's house in Clearwater. (Mrs. Cooper had her trailer in Memphis at the time.) Mrs. Cooper agreed since Cathy's mother was not working for the summer and could help care for Randy, but she reminded Cathy that as soon as Randy regained consciousness, he would want to be with her.

Several weeks passed before Randy became aware of his surroundings. In the meantime, his family realized that he could not hear. Cathy, by instinct, began trying to communicate with him, holding his hand in hers and tracing imaginary letters in space, the way one would teach a small child to write. She wrote lists of his relatives' names, hoping to stimulate his awareness. One day they went riding in her car and he, semiconsciously, directed her to the farmland that his mother owned. After that, Mrs. Cooper moved the trailer back to Clearwater and the couple moved in with her. One afternoon, Randy woke up.

"When I come to on my mom's couch, I couldn't see, I was deaf, I had a broken arm. I tried to think what happened. I couldn't recognize my mom, I couldn't recognize my wife. She said she was my mom, but how could I know. The only thing I could remember, I was seein' and hearin' and goin' around. To give you an idea of how much it did mess me up, I would lay on my couch and pinch myself, thinkin' I was dead, at the waitin' place for someone to come and pick me up. I'd pinch my arm... not dead. This was for 2 or 3 months before I could even think I might still be alive. I can't explain it to you, but... I'm sittin' here talkin' to you, I can see and hear you, and the next thing I know, I can't see or hear. It'll get to ya (laugh)."

The doctors told Randy's family almost nothing about what they could expect, only that some patients do recover their vision and hearing. Cathy said that the doctors seemed frightened to talk with them, for there was nothing certain to say. Randy's mother, having read and heard about other accident cases, told Randy that perhaps he might look forward to getting well. (In fact, he did regain some vision during the first year. Although he quips, "I'm deaf, blind in one eye, and can't see out of the other," he has enough vision in his right eye to see straight ahead about 50 feet, although the image he sees is blurred. He can read signs and fingerspelling, very slowly, about 1 foot from his eye. He can read large print, one letter at a time.)

What his mother told him has been worked into his repertoire of stories: "When I come to on my mom's couch, to know it was me, well, my wife and mother told me the doctor said about 6 months before I get well. Here I am deaf and blind. They told me when the accident happened, it's already been a couple of months; why, only 3 or 4 more and I'll be well. Three or four months passed and I wasn't well. They told me the doctors sometimes have patients for a year before they get well. Six months ain't nothin', a year ain't long. Well, I tell them, Mom, when a year gets here, don't tell me the doctors have some go 2 years. Well, I go across the garden to eat breakfast a lot. After 1 year, I went across the garden one mornin', and she told me the doctors have some go 5 years before they get well. Okay, 5 years. The night before 5 years was here, I went to bed thinkin' I was gonna get up tomorrow and go to the horse races in my truck. The next day when I got up, all I got to do was go out in the garden and pull some 'taters. Now my mom says 7 years. I ain't got but 2 more years and I'll be well."

Randy laughed uproariously as he delivered his punch line, but there is an element of seriousness to the promise that he may see again. (He rarely mentions regaining his hearing.) He has a shadow of faith that he holds on to–and holds on to realistically, despite a lot of talk about "tomorrow" when he is well, not deluding himself. He is aware that it is the hope, the emotion itself, that keeps him going. "In 5 years, I've made a wonderful recovery. Five years ago, I couldn't walk out in the yard by myself. Now I can–I can do things. I can go to town (Clearwater) by myself, walking. I can't drive because I can't see the other people on the road. But to stay on my side walkin' and be careful, I can. I believe to be seein' in 5 years. There's no time limit on it. I mean, I could die like this, just what I can see now. I could have a backslide and go blind. But I will tell you a wonderful thing that God has given me. He has given me my hope. Even if I never do get well, I *hope* I do. I'll tell you somethin' saddenin'–that someone has given up–has no reason to live. In their mind they have no purpose.

"I had one vision in 5 years. In this vision, I seen it as clear as you would look at a book and read it. Skulls and things in a spooky place, and a shack of some sort. I come out of the shack a'smilin' and a'skippin' by them skulls. I'm sittin' up in my bed when I come to myself and I'm sayin', 'Yea, though I walk through the valley of the shadow of death, I will fear no evil . . . .' I still don't understand the vision and my sayin' the prayer at the end. The next day I was walkin' outside by the garden and my nephew come up and said there's a snake there about 4 or 5 feet long; it was dead and didn't have a scratch on it. My wife and little girl walk across that garden to my mom's trailer–and that snake was already dead without a scratch on it.

"I told my vision to a woman where I work. She told me, maybe part of the vision was God tellin' me He was with me. I didn't understand the vision, so He tried a little more with the snake. I believe someone was lookin' out for me when I was close to that snake. When my wife and little girl was walking across the garden, someone was with them, takin' care of them. I believe God was tryin' to tell me that He is with me.

"I can get down and depressed about bein' deaf and blind, but as long as I can look at it and laugh, not worry about it, gettin' well's not all that important. With a job and workin', I'm not missin' nothin'. Missin' drivin' my truck. Hey, that ain't nothin'. I can keep that truck for 10 years if I have to, if it takes me that long to get well."

Randy often contradicts himself, however, when talking about his adjustments to his disabilities and his now-sedentary life. On Tuesday, he believes just what he says about not suffering from what he has lost; on Wednesday, if he can even talk about how he feels, he becomes so perplexed that he stops in mid-sentence, raises his arms, and falls back in his chair. A strange expression often comes across his face; looking at him, you don't know if he is about to laugh or about to cry–then he shakes his head in bewilderment.

Randy is still trying to sort out his life. One day he told me, "The way I was livin' when I hit that fence post, I could very easily be now where I'd sure 'nough be hot. I wasn't livin' for God. The doctors told my mom they couldn't do nothin' for me. I'm on my deathbed, you know. Well, God helped me. In fact, if I hadn't a hit that fence post, I had a case on me in Mississippi, I could'a got 10 years for (laugh). What I'm tryin' to say is, I've got a whole lot to be thankful for. That I'm still here. I'm a lot better off like I am. I'm workin'. I've got a home, a family. I've got two wonderful little girls. I'm not missin' anythin' really."

Yet despite that attitude, Randy is often edgy and moody. He sits around the house for days thinking to himself, sometimes about the past and the present, often "dreaming about tomorrow" when he gets "over that hill."

Randy and Cathy's marriage is difficult for an outsider to understand. They barely knew each other when Randy hit the fence post. Cathy had recently quit her job as a physical education teacher's aide when Randy started to call her. She says they got married for "something to do." She knew of his background, but thought that maybe he would change. I asked Cathy if she thought of leaving Randy after the accident. She answered, "It never crossed my mind." Were they concerned about raising children? "At first, Randy was afraid to have children because he thought they'd be like him. But we told him, no, because he wasn't born with it. We knew, of course, if one of the children was born like that, it wouldn't be because of him. That was the only problem on Randy's mind."

"Now they did a film on Randy for the United Fund a little while ago. A woman came out to interview us and I guess the first question she asked me was, 'What's it like to be the wife of a deaf-blind man? What do I have to do?' I answered her quick. 'I don't do anything more for my husband than you do for yours.' All I have to do is wash his clothes, put his shaving stuff out, fix his meals. Of course, I do the driving.

"Now, well, with Randy laid off, he gets ill-tempered more often. He may sit around for days, sits around and doesn't talk. He doesn't lose his temper that much with me and the kids. He might just tell us, 'Go on out, I want to be by myself.' Most of the time he just sits in his building, shoots pool, or goes and sits out in the yard. (There is a small building behind their house that lodges his pool table, a gift from his mother after the accident.) A lot of times, Randy's depressed and you don't know if it's mad or depressed, but I think, well, I haven't done anything to make him mad, so more likely he's depressed. But he can't stand to sit. He's always got to be doing something."

Although Cathy said she never thought of leaving Randy, three or four times he has told her to go. "It's just when he gets in the mood. What does he say? Just, 'Pack your things and go.' He doesn't holler. We don't have a fight. He just says, 'You go stay with your mom.' If you stayed around here long enough you'd notice that quite a bit of the time Randy mopes. You don't even know when he's in a good mood or a bad mood. He gets, like I said, ill-tempered. Little things get on his nerves. Like Lisa will get in his lap, sit for awhile, get up, come back, get up . . . he gets very ill. Flies off the handle real easy. Usually he just tells her he doesn't feel like messin' with her, and I just have to get on her, make her quit."

"A lot of Randy's illness is I'm with him like I am with the girls. I don't turn over to him. I don't know if Randy's told you, but he's always had everything he wanted. His mother bought him cars, everything. Now his mother, I don't know if you could say she's opened her eyes, but she's starting to see it has hurt Randy more than it has helped. The first year-and-a-half that we was married, I tried to do everything that Randy wanted to do, everything I thought he might want to do. I got to thinkin', well, you know, people can expect too much out of another person.

"I'm working now, but those first few years, we were here together all the time. Mrs. Cooper would say, 'Randy'd be better off if you went to work. Maybe that's what's wrong with him.' So now I'm working, all I hear is, 'It'd be better off to quit.' (Cathy is an inventory clerk for a chain of food stores.) But I know one thing; I won't quit my job. If I quit my job, I'd lose all my sense."

Cathy and Mrs. Cooper have had difficulties, and Cathy agrees with the adage, 'Don't live near your in-laws.' One time when Randy told her to leave, a social worker from the rehabilitation center where Randy was employed came to talk with her. She told the social worker that she had known when they got married that Mrs. Cooper was domineering, but she had not realized how much control his mother had over Randy. Throughout the interviews, Randy would not talk about Cathy, except for one day when he was ornery and complained, with unexpected rancor, about her poor housekeeping. He did, however, continually laud his mother, recounting how she had stuck by him all the time he was in prison, and now that he is deaf and blind. Randy tends to see most family matters from his mother's point of view.

"Now this last time Randy told me to leave, I probably wouldn't have come back if he hadn't called me. A lot of times, I'll leave and come back on my own. The other times I was there only maybe a night. This last time I stayed maybe 2 weeks. You know, in 2 weeks you can get used to living different. You can only take someone telling you to leave so much.

"But I'll stay with Randy as long as he acts like he wants us here and expects to give as much as he expects to take. This last time he told us to leave, he had it in his mind that he could make it fine on his own—that he was capable of taking care of himself. A nephew of Randy's—I found this out later—told him once if I leave, he'd move in with him. Randy had it in his mind that if I left and this nephew moves in, he can go anywhere he wants to.

"I don't know how Randy feels about wishing he never got married. I don't regret it. His ill temper gets to me, but I just walk off, do my work and I'm all right. This all don't have anything to do with Randy's being deaf and blind. We're just a typical couple with typical problems. I don't think we have more problems than any other couple. It's just life to have problems, fusses, fights. If I thought Randy hated me or I hated Randy, I wouldn't be here."

Randy was at home all day, every day, for 2 years following his accident. Although Cathy contacted vocational rehabilitation early and he began receiving disability payments, he did not enter a training or work program until 1975. Neither Randy nor Cathy can recall the reason for the delay, although Cathy did say that there was a period of time when Randy refused to go anywhere. After a job evaluation in 1975, he started working at the rehabilitation center's sheltered workshop in Memphis, operating machinery that attaches snaps to knapsacks; he worked on contracts from a local U.S. Army post. After a few months, his vocational rehabilitation counselor arranged for him and his family to move to Chattanooga and live in a trailer while he attended the state vocational-technical school for the deaf. Larry agreed to go only after his mother persuaded him, but he maintained that he did not want to leave her alone.

In Chattanooga, he and Cathy began learning sign language and fingerspelling, and they continue to study it on their own, although both she and his mother usually communicate with him by printing letters on his arm, a very slow process. He also started to learn Braille, but he found it frustrating and quit. He rejected a cane and mobility training, just as he still prefers to follow behind another person, rather than to be guided by holding an arm.

Randy stayed in Chattanooga only 1 month before packing up and going home, informing the manager of the trailer park of his departure, but not letting the school know that he was quitting. He says the school was not prepared for his arrival, and he could not cope with having to "sit and wait, sit and wait" most of the time. In addition to the inactivity, Randy says he left because his mother needed him. It might have been the other way around. His vocational rehabilitation counselor suggests, too, that Randy had difficulty leaving the workshop where, because of his charisma and the severity of his disabilities, he had become the unofficial "Mr. Rehabilitation Center."

Back in Memphis, he was reaccepted for his old job and continued to work for 2½ years until the Army contract for which he had been hired expired. A new one has not yet been negotiated, and although his vocational rehabilitation counselor keeps trying to find him a job, and he and Cathy have looked on their own, he has been unemployed for 3 months. For awhile he made leather wallets and key purses, but selling them was difficult. He was offered a job tossing cotton into a gin, but he would have lost his Supplemental Security Income (S.S.I.) benefits, including Medicare, if he accepted it. The salary would not have been large enough to make up for them. The family has been living on Cathy's small income, even less significant Aid to Dependent Children payments, loans from their parents, and his S.S.I.

Having to depend on S.S.I. enrages Randy. His attitude toward work has changed considerably from his days as a convict. "You know, after the accident, I could sit here at home and try to think of something to do. Couldn't. There wasn't nothing I could do. Things that needed doin', I couldn't do. It'd just build up on me. Then I got to go to work. Believe me, workin' and drawin' a paycheck every Friday—then there ain't nothin' wrong with me. I mean I'm workin', makin' a livin'. Somebody's not givin' it to me. I'm not charity when I'm workin'. I'm a little under it right now, but when I get to workin' again...."

"S.S.I. sent me a letter when I got off from work. 'We're gonna give you $168 a month.' The next week they sent me a letter, 'You have overdrawn $2,300; you owe us $2,300.' I don't know if I'm goin' or comin'. They sent me a letter last week, 'We're gonna give you $180 a month.' They sent me $115 this month. Oooh, if I ever get me a job ... why I don't need 'em. That's one goal I have in the future–gettin' off these damned.... Draw a paycheck on Friday, I work for it, I can spend it the way I want to. I ain't got to worry about my boss man sayin', 'I overpaid you last week.' I ain't got to worry about goin' down, tellin' S.S.I. what I done last month. All I gotta worry is gettin' up and goin' to work.

"There's only one thing anybody can do for me. That's gettin' me a job that is mine to keep as long as I do my work and do it right. Any kind of job. I don't care what. Anything. I'll tell you, if it weren't for Pumpkin and Laurie, I've got a little thing I'd tell to those people at S.S.I. and Welfare. But you can't make two little girls suffer for your dumbness."

The more Randy talked about this, the angrier he became. Cathy had said that thinking about S.S.I. puts Randy in such a mood that nobody wants to be around him. He continued, "I'm not crazy about work. I just want to make a livin', earn money, draw a paycheck, spend it the way I want to. Somebody ask me how I spent my paycheck, that's my business. If I want to tell, I can. If I don't, I won't."

"Let me tell you the whole answer to the problem. I believe I'm gonna get well again. Today I'm slidin'. You want to kick me, kick me today. Next week when I'm well, be two-sided then, won't be one-sided. Now I haven't got no choice. I am told what I am wanted to know, that's all. I'm not told what I *want* to know. You take a person in my condition—just make do, just get by. You can call it crazy or what you will, but if I come to the conclusion that I'm not gonna see again, you don't have to worry about writin' nothin' about me unless you be writin' my obituary. I would just check out on the other side. See if what's supposed to be there is there."

Randy was speaking in anger, but even when he is not so upset he expresses the same feelings about what he would do if he lost his hope. He has also considered how he would feel if he were totally blind. "I'm deaf and almost blind now, but I can see to move around. If I were completely blind, the police could not do one thing to hurt me. If they arrested me, the only thing I'd do is holler, 'Feed me, I'm hungry.' But when you can see, you sort of like to be out where you can move around. I think I would meet the Maker if everytime I went out in the yard I had to ask somebody to lead me."

Randy values his freedom to move, but he is also concerned with the self-sufficiency that it implies. Independence and dependence are issues that he is dealing with. He has some interesting habits: in addition to the car that they bought when Cathy started working, the couple owns a truck, "my truck" as Randy always refers to it. Although he cannot drive it, he will not let Cathy keep the keys. He becomes almost belligerent when someone suggests that he may be dependent on other people for help, and then he puts his response in financial terms. "Dependent—what for? Nelson (Gene Nelson, Randy's vocational rehabilitation counselor) gets me a job, I won't be dependent on nobody. You get grocery money this week; if I work, draw a paycheck, I'll be eatin' next week, too. You don't have to give me nothin'." When he is in a different mood, however, he says, "You're right. I have to depend on people. I have to depend on other people too much."

"It hurts sometimes not being able to go see somebody about somethin' myself. I have friends, mechanics and things out in the country. I can't go and pass a few minutes with them, talkin' or somethin'. I have to get somebody else to go with me. I can't get to town to look for a job myself. My wife works ... probably nobody'd harm me, but when I could see and hear and I went lookin' for a job, I got it, I found one. I can't do that now. Just sit here at the house.

"It's the same as in prison—your biggest problem, or mine anyway, has been realizin' the things I can do and the things I can't. I'd jump up and want to do things. I'd go to the horse races if I could drive. That's what I do miss. Ridin'. Goin' nowhere. You and another guy or a coupl'a more guys just havin' fun, just laughin'. I'm not thinkin' of goin' to other states. I'm talkin' about in town, right here in the country, just ridin' around yourself, seein' other people."

Until recently, Randy's two daughters from his first marriage have stayed with him on weekends, but the older girl decided that she wanted to live with Randy and Cathy, and her mother put an end to the visits. He has other relatives living nearby in the country, but they rarely come to see him. He becomes bitter about his sisters' being too *busy* (he says it sarcastically) to visit, although he usually chastises them for neglecting their mother, not him. When he first got the pool table, his teenaged cousins were at the house day and night, but their visits have tapered off. About his other cousins and acquaintances he says, "When I get my vision back, I'll have friends. Oooh. Happy to see me. Probably wanna buy me a drink. They didn' worry about seein' me the 5 years I was deaf and blind. Don't any of 'em stop by, say,

'Hi, How ya doin?' I'm deaf and blind. I don't call 'em friends; friends are hard to come by."

A few times a year, someone does visit, bringing liquor, and Randy drinks. Usually outsiders get him started, although sometimes he just decides to get drunk. "When my cousin comes by, I drink social, you know. But when things get to me, I drink myself. Thing's build up on me. You want to get even and you can't. But it don't straighten nothin' out. The doctor told me I'd have to stop drinkin' or it'd take me longer to get well. No drinkin'." A couple of months ago, however, he did get drunk, and wanted to go into town. "Cathy wouldn't take me. Mom wouldn't take me. Got in my truck and I'm goin' to town. I didn't even get to the road. I hit the ditch over there. Just sank down. I didn't try that but one time. Nelson came over and talked to me about it. He told me I had to give up drivin'. I told him it was a hard habit, but I guess I could. I told him I walked about 4 or 5 miles into town. He said I didn't have to quit that; told me it's good for me." After that, Randy fashioned himself a cane, his walking stick, from a pool stick; he cut off the bottom and attached a rubber tip. He uses it now when he goes away from home.

Both Randy and Cathy get along well with Gene Nelson. Two or three times a week, Randy calls him at the office or at his home, whenever he feels that he needs a friend to talk with. Gene has told Randy that he does not have to act or pretend, he can just be himself, and Randy feels comfortable letting Gene see his two kinds of "craziness"–the elements of the old Randy, growing a stubby beard and finding a big straw hat just to go down to the center and laugh with Gene; and the newer confusion, when he feels depressed and calls Gene saying, "I'm in one of them old crazy moods again," then asks if Gene really thinks he should learn Braille, or should he try to get a job at this place or that, talking until he and Gene start joking and Randy begins to feel better.

Randy so frequently mentioned the future when he gets his vision back that I asked him what he would do. He answered, "If I woke up in the morning and I could see, all our talks would be a hill of beans. I don't know what I'd do. I have lived by brainstorms. I'm sittin' here and somebody mentions Illinois. I've got a cousin who lives in Illinois. Up and go. Brainstorms. Your brain starts jumpin' up and down with an idea. I cannot sit here and tell you if I'd get a job, work for a livin', straighten up, or go back to outlaw. I've had things happen to me since I've been like this . . . . But I'll tell you a wonderful thing. There are people, I suppose in all towns, like at the center down there, Nelson, Ann, Rita. If you want help, you can get it."

"You want the truth? I'm not speakin' now of bein' brave or somethin'. I'm speakin' of livin'. Whatever happens, go with it. I can be sittin' here at the house, get mad about somethin'. Sure 'nough mad and there's nothin' I can do about it in my condition. And Pumpkin or Laurie will come runnin' through the house and take and hug my leg, take and hug my leg for no reason. I don't know what's gonna happen to me. But the important thing is God has let me keep my hope. As long as I have it, if I have hope when I die, deaf-blind won't matter, won't mean nothin'. Next year, or the next year, or the next year . . . ."

Bill Moore*

The effects of Bill Moore's isolation show on his face. The first night we** went to his house to interview him, an almost fierce-looking man opened the door. All of his face frowned and he seemed frozen in that frown. His eyes were closed and the heavy bags under them ran into the scowling lines of his cheeks and jaws. He looked hard and mean and ugly. His behavior and his language also reflected years of loneliness and anger.

We had specific preliminary questions to ask before beginning the interviews, but he paid no attention to us. He had covered our hands to read our signs and fingerspelling tactually when we greeted him. When he started signing, after us, but not in response to us, he kept his grip on our hands. He signed on and on, almost furiously, ignoring our attempts to interrupt, ask for clarification, or change the subject. When we tried to extract our hands, he tightened his hold. He jumped from one topic to another, one time period to another, without making connections for us. Even with an intermediary interpreter, another deaf man, we could not understand crucial parts of what he was relating. His signs were sometimes inexact and his fingerspelling stiff, but more confusing than that, he did not use American Sign Language (A.S.L.) in the standard way–he did not employ the space around him to differentiate persons, places,

*The names have been changed.
**two interpreters and the writer

and times; he did not identify for us the similar name signs that he used for different people. He was a man talking to himself but demanding an audience to stay with him.

Our interviews for the next three nights were basically the same. He told mostly about his divorce and confinement in jail 20 years ago, and the taunting he had experienced at Goodwill Industries 2 years ago. But from his manner of expressing himself—his intensity, his anger, and his limited explanation of *who* and *when*—we had only a vague understanding of the details and chronology of the events in his life; we found we had to contact relatives, agency workers, and members of the deaf community in his city even to postulate a coherent account of his experiences.

Bill has Usher's Syndrome, a genetic condition with the predominant symptoms of hearing loss and vision impairment. It is characterized by deafness or lesser hearing loss, most often present at birth, accompanied by a specific restriction of vision due to *retinitis pigmentosa*. *Retinitis pigmentosa* causes slow deterioration of the retina, resulting in early night blindness and progressive loss of peripheral vision. According to government statistics, Usher's Syndrome is the most common cause of deaf-blindness; those with it, the largest population of deaf-blind adults. Yet, as a group, they are the hardest people for agencies and, often, their families and friends to deal with.

Unlike those who lose their hearing after developing speech and English language patterns, most people with Usher's Syndrome have as their first and only language, A.S.L. They may comprehend simple English constructions and have some English vocabulary, but extensive, clear, and satisfying communication with a person who does not know A.S.L. may be impossible.

Socially, although it would seem that the deaf individual who becomes blind could continue to associate with sighted-deaf people sharing the same language and, some would say, world-view, that is reportedly rarely the case. Those who work with the deaf, and deaf-blind people themselves, hold it as a truism that deaf people ignore the deaf-blind. They explain that the deaf person, having grown up dependent upon eyesight for communication and for the freedom to play sports, drive, and travel freely, thinks blindness a deplorable handicap and pities the blind person. To be deaf and lose one's vision, some claim, is the deaf person's greatest fear. When it happens to someone else, particularly in the gradual and unexplained pattern of Usher's Syndrome, the sighted-deaf person's reaction is an avoidance of that individual, a shunning from the confrontation with the nagging feeling, "It could happen to me." The axiom goes, "The deaf ignore the deaf-blind," and both it and the suggested underlying psychological motivation may be largely accurate. But the axiom does not acknowledge the multiple and intertwining threads in any individual's life—the timing of events, the person's personality and preferences—that may also determine the course of his experiences. The theory does not grapple with the disturbing possibility that the deaf-blind person's loss of contact, though nonetheless painful, may also be a drifting away; the deaf community's reaction, a forgetting rather than an abrupt and callous rejection.

Bill has always been something of a loner. He was born on a farm outside of a small southern city. His mother had been a widow when she married his father, and his half-sister, Arlene, was 11 when he was born. Bill's deafness was not discovered until he was 3 years old. Arlene explains that neither her stepfather nor her mother had had enough recent contact with infants to notice that Bill did not respond to sounds or begin to develop speech at a normal age. Neighbors, however, were concerned and urged his parents to consult a physician in town. The doctor told them that their son had been born deaf, would always be deaf, and there was nothing to be done about it. With that scant advice, the Moore family returned to the farm.

When Bill was 6 years old, the family moved to the city and found a small house surrounded by a large plot of land at the rural northern end. It was the beginning of the Depression, and until he found a chemical plant job through the Work Projects Administration, Bill's father was unemployed. There was no school for the deaf in town at the time, and again Bill stayed at home. Arlene recalls that Mr. Moore, already in his forties and tending to overprotect his young son, was hesitant to send him to the state residential school for the deaf 200 miles away; Bill's understanding is that he had no schooling simply because the family had no money.

There were other boys on the street and Bill played with them. His early methods of communication and the satisfaction or frustration that he experienced can only be guessed at now, for neither he nor Arlene seem to recall. All indications from them are that he was a well-loved, happy child; an old photograph reveals a sweet, serene face. Somewhat isolated for reasons of geography and the economics of the period, and even more sheltered because of his parents' protective attitude, he seems to have grown up a quiet, agreeable boy, easy to get along with and content with what to many people would be disturbingly restricted contact with others.

When Bill was 9, his sister Agnes was born. Now alert to early symptoms, his parents quickly recognized that she, too, was deaf. When Bill was 11, a school department official visited his home and informed his parents that he must be enrolled in the classroom for deaf children that had been established at a local public school. He learned fingerspelling there and some signs from other children, but the program was oral in philosophy and concentrated on lipreading and speech training. After 4 years, during which Bill probably did not do very well considering the age at which he began, a teacher told Mr. Moore that he would have to send the boy to the state school to learn a vocation for, after all, Mr. Moore would not be around to take care of Bill forever. Though still apprehensive, his father sent both Bill and Agnes to live away from home.

Bill entered the school's vocational program where he learned the trade of woolpressing. He did not have close friends, but he sometimes participated with his classmates in outings and parties. He had a couple of girlfriends, among them, Laura Johnson, whom he later married. When Bill was 20, he injured his back. He left school for two operations he needed and did not return to graduate. Instead, he moved back home with his parents and found a job as a woolpresser. A few years later, when he was 23, he married Laura. His father gave the couple some land next to his own home and Bill had a house built.

People who knew Bill as a young man recall that he was pleasant. He knew his neighbors and communicated with them using pencil and paper. They say that he was a quiet man both before and during his marriage. He had acquaintances in the deaf community, many of whom had also been at the state school. Until the mid-nineteen fifties, he and Laura attended local church services interpreted into sign language for the sizable deaf membership of the congregation. Bill, however, became frustrated by the poor interpreting available and stopped going to church. When most of the other deaf members also left in anger, but reorganized at another church, Bill and Laura did not follow.

Bill sometimes joined other deaf people in social activities—primarily going to the deaf club on Saturday night, although on one occasion he rode with a group to the state association of the deaf's weekend get-together—but Laura did not usually accompany him. Bill found that he did not enjoy too much socializing: "Drinking, parties, clubs—I got tired of it. Better to go once in a while." After they had been married 9 years, Laura had a son, and presumably Bill was content to stay home with his family and visit his parents nearby, a not uncommon pattern for young deaf couples in his town at that time. A bit later in his life, when his vision began to deteriorate quickly, he may have passed from limited inclination to see other people to lost opportunity for initiating social contact.

When he reached his early thirties, Bill's life began to change rapidly. Within a few years, he lost his usable vision, his family, and his work. Bill recounts the events of the period as merely coincidental and not related causally. Other people, however—his sisters and former neighbors—feel certain that vision problems led to the initial job loss and his inability to retain further employment. Although no one mentions the possibility, his sight problems may also have, at least subtly, affected his relationship with Laura or her family's feeling about Bill's worth as a husband.

The period of his life most vivid to him now, the events that he poured out over and over again in our early interviews, occurred 20 years ago. In 1957, when Bill was 33, Laura left him. A year later, after long and bitter litigation, she was granted a divorce in the county where her parents lived and seem to have had some influence. She received custody of their 2-year-old son, an award of $15 a week for child support, and rental rights to the house the couple owned. They had been married 11 years. According to Bill, they had gotten along well enough until the last few years when he could not tolerate her neglect of housework and bill-paying, or her frequent extended visits to her parents' house 90 miles away. Bill says that Laura had been very spoiled by her parents, always depending on "daddy, daddy, daddy." Early in their marriage she had developed the habit of spending a week or 2 at her parents' house every month or 2, her parents providing the transportation and, Bill believes, considerable encouragement. By the late fifties she was "back and forth, back and forth, every 2 weeks." Bill's frustration mounted to the point where, occasionally–three or four times in all–he slapped her face. Laura filed for divorce on the grounds of wife beating. The trial, however, centered around her accusation that Bill never provided her with food. Neighbors swarmed to the distant courthouse to support Bill as character witnesses and to testify that, in fact, he regularly brought home bagfuls of groceries, transporting them in taxicabs for Bill could not drive and the couple had no car. It was, in addition, a dubious allegation from a rather hefty woman.

The divorce left Bill shattered. Though it was no longer a happy marriage–and there was some talk that the child was not his—Bill wanted his wife and son. Aware of the influ- his in-laws held on Laura, he must have realized that to continue a relationship with her in any form would be impossible. Had he guessed that he would never see his son again, he would no doubt have been even more depressed than he was. With the loss of the home for which, just two years before, he had made the final mortgage payment, Bill moved into his parents' house next door.

In September 1958, 4 months after the divorce was granted, Bill lost his cleaning company job. He explains simply that racial patterns in the city were shifting; with the influx of more Blacks who could be paid lower wages, white employees were laid off. When his company was sold and the new owners dismissed him, Bill's mother called to find out why. Apparently she did not provide him with satisfactory answers, for today he still resents the secret telephoning and gossiping his parents were engaged in at about that time. Bill searched for other jobs, but found only temporary employment. Two different cleaning establishments hired him, then laid him off rapidly. A third company kept him on longer, not as a presser, but to do janitorial work. When he was dismissed from this last job, Bill was left with little to do all day. He visited with a deaf woman living across the street, pouring out his miseries over the divorce. He spent the rest of his time sitting in his parents' house, crying. When his deaf sister, with whom he had been close, came to visit, he walked into his room and slammed the door.

At about the same time as his divorce and his adjustment to unemployment, Bill was losing his vision. His own recollections of the deterioration are vague, as are the memories of other family members and existing medical records from that period. Bill attributes the loss to a number of different causes. In 1957 he had had a bad cold and his vision began to blur. After the divorce he cried endlessly and his vision deteriorated rapidly. At some point he was punched in the head and near one eye by angry in-laws. He says, too, that he was once given medication to calm him down, and that contributed to his eventual blindness.

Agnes and Arlene both refer to his depression and constant crying after the divorce as at least hastening the loss. Arlene once got the impression, too, probably from a doctor, that Bill had burst blood vessels in his eyes. An old social service agency record cites "numerous eye disorders and the retina wasting away."

The husband of the deaf woman whom Bill visited after his divorce, a neighbor for many years, recalls that Bill had had vision problems for a long time. During the last year of Bill's marriage, when that neighbor married and brought his wife to live across the street, the woman noticed that Bill had tunnel vision. He bumped into parked cars; he could not see hands waving at his side for his attention; when he entered their house, moving from the bright outdoors to the more dimly lit interior, he faltered and stumbled. All are signs of *retinitis pigmentosa* and, indeed, in a recent medical examination, a doctor finally confirmed that diagnosis. Bill, however, does not recall early night blindness or the gradual loss of peripheral vision, the two very specific symptoms of the disease.

After the divorce, with no success in finding steady work, Bill stayed at home for almost 3 years. His father paid the child support until an illness left him bedridden. At that point, Bill's mother refused to continue payments to her son's ex-wife who was already receiving an income from the divorced couple's property. In September 1960, Bill was summoned to his wife's home county charged with contempt of court for neglecting the payments for 40 weeks. He and his family were not informed that he had the right to postpone appearance for up to 10 days to secure a lawyer. His mother, with his half-sister and her husband, accompanied him to court, where his former wife's family and, it appears, the court officials attempted to coerce him into granting Laura sole ownership of the property she already controlled. The Moores refused to comply and returned home.

On December 30, 1960, with no warning, the sheriff's men from his ex-wife's county seized him from his parents' home and jailed him. It was probably then that his former brother-in-law and father-in-law struck him in anger; the sheriff's men may also have given him some medication as a tranquilizer. His mother alerted his half-sister of the situation and Arlene hired a lawyer. With a writ of *habeaus corpus*, they secured Bill's release, but not until January 3rd, the next business day. Bill's lawyer filed suit in the State Supreme Court resulting eventually in the charges against Bill being dropped. Again, the condition of his vision at the time is unclear. The court records for February 1961 describe Bill as a "deaf-mute," with no reference to impaired vision. His half-sister, Arlene, thinks he was blind or nearly blind; Bill says only that he could see.

In January 1961, Bill's father had died, followed in August by his mother. There were suspicions about Arlene's role in the division of their property, causing a bitterness that has continued to this day. Each of the three siblings describes the situation differently. In any event, Arlene had a two-and-a-half room house built for Bill–adjacent to the other houses he had lived in on the property their parents had owned. Agnes, feeling she did not receive a share of the inheritance equal to that of her half-sister and angry that her brother had gotten a house, disappeared from their lives for some 6 or 7 years.

After his parents' deaths, Arlene, his hearing half-sister, assumed greater responsibility for Bill. She accompanied him to doctors' appointments, interpreting, as she and her parents had communicated with him all of his life, either through notes or by printing letters on his palm. One eye doctor recommended that they contact the state commission for the blind. Records from 1961 show that Bill's vision was 20/200, corrected with glasses to 20/30. The records also refer to a peripheral loss, but say only that, because of his poor acuity, it was immeasurable.

In November 1961, with Arlene continuing as interpreter in all meetings, the commission placed Bill in a Lighthouse for the Blind in another city. He was trained in sewing, assembly work, and broom-making and worked in their laundry, folding and counting pillow-cases. He stayed for 3 months' training before returning home. He was unemployed briefly before his placement in a local Lighthouse, assembling and packing pens. At one time, he wrote to the Lighthouse where he had been trained asking for his position back and inquiring about people he had known there. For a year or 2 he worked in his hometown, sometimes steadily, frequently on and off. Records indicate that his employment at the second Lighthouse was terminated because of a shortage of work. From 1965 to 1968, Bill had no work at all, and again he just sat at home all day. Interestingly, though he had had some training and work between 1958 and 1968, Bill counts that time as a 10-year period of unemployment. He says, too, thinking back from 1978, that he has been totally blind for 13 years, or since 1965. According to Arlene, that last period of unemployment was a frightening time for him; on the few occasions that he went out, he became lost in the city trying to change buses. She says that he was confused and disorganized in managing his house. One evening, a drunken man or thief attempted to break in. Neighbors, alerted by the commotion, called her, and Bill stayed at her home for a week until he was calm enough to return to his own house.

In 1968, the commission for the blind arranged for Bill to enter the rehabilitation program for deaf-blind individuals at the Industrial Home for the Blind in Brooklyn, New York. He stayed for a total of 12 weeks of training in independent travel using public transportation, daily living skills such as cooking, and, after an evaluation of his skills, assembly work for future employment. He also had instruction in communication methods–Braille, fingerspelling, palm printing, and handwriting. He returned home and was placed in a job at Goodwill.

For the past 10 years he has worked in a number of different departments there, most recently polishing furniture and counting clothes hangers. Except for a deaf woman, Miss H, who worked there briefly a few years ago, and a truck driver who is rarely in the building, Bill is the only deaf employee. He has not been happy, primarily because there is not enough work for him to do. Goodwill sometimes sends people home early in the day, or cuts working hours down to three days a week. At other times they have given Bill "busy work" like stringing beads instead of sending him home. When either situation occurs he signs to himself furiously and makes sounds that are unmistakable in tone.
    He has had other difficulties at Goodwill–one connected with his paychecks. Different departments pay different wages and, since he has been shifted among departments, his paycheck is not always the same. The problem itself seems to be that there is not always adequate communication between Bill and the supervisory personnel at Goodwill. They do not clearly explain what is happening to him and he allows his confusion and anger to build up. At the point when he makes a lot of noise and gestures angrily, Goodwill calls in an interpreter who knows sign language.
    Over his shirt pocket he wears a large pin that says "Boss" in bold letters; taped onto it is his name. Someone gave him the pin in New York and he is proud of it–it means that he cannot be pushed around. Yet he had trouble at Goodwill a year-and-a-half ago when some emotionally-disturbed teenagers were brought there to work. The group of them taunted Bill, poking and punching him when he was trying to work. Their badgering continued for weeks until he became so angry that he grabbed one boy and banged his head against the wall; he threw a chair at another. Goodwill brought in an interpreter to explain to Bill that the teenagers were emotionally-disturbed, but the problem was not resolved until they were placed elsewhere. The supervisors at Goodwill who know Bill think that his frustration in that situation was justified; they talk about him with genuine affection, saying that he is a sweet man.
    Bill generally eats alone, although sometimes a supervisor will sit down with him at lunchtime and print into his palm. When people do attempt to communicate with him, he starts signing and does not want to let them go. He writes

letters addressed to "Goodwill" regularly. Although he has a wire device to guide his pen on a straight line, his handwriting is difficult to read and his grammar is a blend of English and A.S.L. A few years ago, after the deaf woman with whom he would eat lunch and chat left, he sent Goodwill this letter:

> "look to work today. How are you doing? I write you today. I cook some roast beef with dressing this a.m. and green beans with pie and jello. Fine, very good, same. Why little Miss H. not like much move. Can you drive car? Blind Bill are working at Goodwill. I want to get married to Miss H. this year. Do you love blind Bill very good? Bill working at the bags. Do you like to work at Goodwill?"

Bill goes to work on the bus every day, transferring once downtown. He walks to and from the end points and inside Goodwill independently with a cane, but at his transfer points he uses cards to ask people for help. He has a set of cards that reads, "I am deaf and blind" and requests aid to different corners and buses. He identifies the appropriate card for each transfer by the number of staples at the top. Some people ignore him when he presents his card while others, he can sense, bristle in fear. He thinks that they are silly to be afraid of him and is much less annoyed by them than he is by the people on the bus who push and shove and rest their feet in the aisles. When strangers on the street respond to his cards and help him, he must often bear with their inexperienced techniques as sighted guides. That is bothersome, too, and can be dangerous for him, but he tries to be patient and to correct them by gesturing that they must raise and lower their arms enough to warn him that he is approaching a curb. In the past he has had to cope with bus drivers who forget to tap him when they have reached the destination indicated on his card, but he has been riding for so long on the same route that he can feel the familiar turns and road textures well enough to know most of the time when to get off.

Bill's half-sister and her husband have helped him with some of his chores since his parents died. Arlene takes him to the barber when necessary and to the grocery store every two weeks. He keeps a list of what he needs; as they walk down the aisles, she palm prints the items from his list and he takes them himself from the shelves and bins. Arlene also helps him with his bills. She says she learned some years ago that he was sending money to the utility companies without knowing the amounts of either the bills or of the money he was enclosing; at that point, she took over, having his bills sent to her home and withdrawing money from his bank account. Bill says, rather, that as part of their weekend chores, *he* pays the bills personally, accompanied by Arlene.

He spends holidays and his birthday at Arlene's home with her family and her friends. In recent years his deaf sister, Agnes, has been in contact with the family again and she and her children also gather at Arlene's house for the holidays. Although Agnes says that she feels awkward around Bill and cannot understand him, Arlene says that when the two of them are there, they sit together signing all afternoon.

It seems that his contact with his relatives has enabled Bill to maintain a cognizance of outside affairs. He is aware of new buildings in his town and is interested in the features of different makes of automobiles. From Agnes he learned that his son had graduated from college and had been married and divorced. Bill likes to hear about Arlene's husband's work and that of his nieces and nephews. On holidays, he plays with Arlene's grandchildren. Last Christmas he gave Agnes' daughter a vase that had been his mother's. When the city's subway system was renovated a year ago, Arlene took him for a ride on it.

Bill is not satisfied with these relationships, however. He likes Agnes–his deaf sister who does nothing for him–and he wishes that she would visit. But he complains about Arlene and says that he hates her husband. Though Lloyd takes care of his yard for him, Bill says he is lazy, letting the grass grow too long before cutting it. His most bitter complaint against his brother-in-law, however, seems to be that Lloyd has never wanted to learn to communicate with his deaf relatives. Instead he always "hides with his nose in a book." Bill claims that Arlene steals his money. When he goes to the store she tells him the prices. Later, he says, when he asks for an accounting of the merchandise, item by item, she prints vaguely and sloppily into his palm and, one way or another, puts off his questions. About his half-sister and his trouble at Goodwill, he says, "All this trouble, and my eyes being ruined, all this trouble. But I have been patient all these years, through this all 16 years. But later I'm going to get a lawyer. They're all crazy. I'm just trying to be friendly, love."

The 16 years that he mentions refers to the amount of time that has passed without any deaf people coming to see him. Bill says that he is lonely and he has told Arlene more than once that when he dies he does not want to be buried way out in the country cemetery where his parents are. After work every day he cooks dinner, writes letters, and goes to bed. He cannot read Braille very well so he does not read newspapers, although formerly he was very much interested in current events. When he does not go shopping with Arlene on Saturdays, he sits inside his house. On Sundays he sleeps all day. His perception of his loneliness is that he has been deserted by the deaf community. He believes that Miss H., the deaf woman he had known for a few months at Goodwill, declined his marriage proposal only because he is blind. Bill wants to marry again, and he feels the left-hand ring finger of every woman he meets. He wants to find a sighted woman who will be able to drive him around, interpret for him in church, and, most importantly, love him in spite of his blindness. He signs, more or less resignedly, that no deaf people have visited him for 16 years. But he is bitter in his charge that the reason that they do not care; that he is "thumbs down," worthless, warranting rejection, is his blindness.

Although he writes frequent letters to Goodwill and to the neighbors who have lived on his street for 35 years, the only letters that he told us about himself are the few that he wrote to a deaf man 3 or 4 years ago. The man had been a friend in the fifties, perhaps too close a friend of Arlene's for Bill's taste, for Bill had once told him to leave his house and never come back. His more recent letters have implored the man to visit, but Bill has heard no response.

We interviewed Bill one afternoon at the local center for the deaf. It was the day of the weekly senior citizen gathering there and, as we left the building, several people recognized Bill. They were surprised to see him; it had been 20 years. The older people were milling about, waiting for the center's station wagon to take them home. As one or two of them went over to Bill, the others stood on the fringes, half watching as they talked animatedly with us and with each other about Bill. One man remarked to his wife, "I used to work with him at Monroe's, 25 years ago." "Bill Moore," she replied, shaking her head, "I thought he'd moved away." As we stood there, more and more of the senior citizens entered a casual but discernible line to talk with Bill. As each person introduced himself, Bill nodded his head, a habit both when he understands and does not understand. But he seemed to pay attention as other people signed to him.

By that afternoon, we had interviewed Bill six times. For the first four nights, he had spilled out, over and over again, the same descriptions, the same emotion-charged accounts of the indignities he had suffered, interspersed with other autobiographical information, but overpowering it.

Then something happened. Bill calmed down. He loosened his grip on our hands–not much, but perceptibly. He still signed at length and his meanings were not altogether clear, but there was a new aspect to our communication. We began to have conversations. We could see Bill's concentration as he tried to read and understand our signs. When we fingerspelled to him, he had us form each letter slowly and separately and he felt our hands carefully. His face relaxed; the tight lines eased. He opened his eyes more frequently as he signed and especially as he listened. When he knew he was signing to a hearing person, he used his voice, too. After 12 hours of telling his frustration–signing his frustration– to people whom he assumed could understand him and, it seemed, particularly to another deaf person, the intermediary interpreter, a gentle, kind, and gracious personality began to emerge.

The last night that we interviewed Bill, we told him that the deaf man who had been interpreting wanted to take him to the deaf club on Saturday night. Bill agreed to go. When we told him to bring some money for refreshments and wear a nice shirt, he teased us, asking, "Do you think I am sweet?" On Saturday night, before he arrived at the deaf club, several people were there who had known him, including the husband and wife who had lived across the street and another couple who had lived around the corner. They all had heard Bill was coming, and one woman mused, "I want to see Bill." He came in with the man who had driven him, scented with after-shave lotion and wearing a suit. One woman came over to say hello, and they had a long conversation as Bill told her about his training and work for the past 20 years. They were interrupted for the business meeting, during which the man who had brought Bill interpreted for him. Bill's face was relaxed all evening and he was gracious. He laughed a few times during the meeting, amused by the debates on the floor. Afterwards, he talked with one or two more people, still monopolizing conversations but listening, too, to other people when they indicated that they wanted to tell him about their lives. His signing was smooth, his hands on other people's hands far gentler than they had been 2 weeks before. There was no tremendous fanfare at the deaf club, no sudden and arresting change in people's interest in Bill's future. But a short time before, Bill had seemed like an old grandfather recounting the old days, a Rip Van Winkle stuck in the morass of his divorce and ensuing difficulties. By now, Bill's grasp of what has happened in his hometown and in the lives of the people who have maintained contact with him was obvious—as obvious as his thirst to catch up on what he has missed for 20 years.

Lucian Cordaro

"There's an interesting thing—linguistically—in Sicilian. I remember my parents and other people I knew referring to people who had something happen to them, some tragic occurrence like an accident or a stroke or some kind of disability. They used the term *disgrazia*. *Disgrazia* means *disgrace*. A negative judgment is implied.

"I want to get into a little psychological theory on this. If someone looks at me—deafness and blindness—there's a negative reaction. In some psychological theories, if there's a negative effect, it has to have a negative cause—just from a standpoint of avoiding incongruity in our systems. Otherwise we'd have dissonance. You have to do something to get your system back in balance. It's the stuff that prejudice is made of. The message that I've received, implicitly, is that when you have something wrong with you, that's not okay. If someone treats me like it's not okay, I have to think, oh, deafness, blindness, they're bad and therefore I'm inadequate.

"Historically speaking, if you look at mythology and literature, the blind have always been prophets or pariahs; there's no middle ground. It's kind of like when I had to deal with my blindness, my choices were invalid or Superman—take your choice. So I went the Superman route."

Lou Cordaro is a clinical psychologist. He lives alone in a comfortable apartment near the fashionable shopping district of Kansas City, Missouri. In many ways, he seems out of place in the conservative Midwest: he has been thrice married and divorced; his grey hair is somewhat longer than what local standards dictate; he talks of "owning" his feelings, "sharing" his thoughts, and the woman whom he is currently "relating to." Although he dislikes labels, he would probably agree that he is a humanistic psychologist. He believes, both in his work and in his personal life, in accepting feelings, exploring them, and, when necessary, "getting them out." He speaks candidly of his mourning for the abilities and the sense of himself lost through his disabilities; of despair; of grieving until his body has been "wracked with sobs." He speaks, too, of the adjustments he has made, the support and friendships he has built, and the pleasures he enjoys.

Lou is 48 years old. He is partially-sighted and hard-of-hearing as a result of glaucoma and Meniere's Syndrome respectively. The glaucoma was discovered when he was 21 and his right eye was replaced by a prosthesis when he was 26. The central vision in his left eye is blocked by a *scotoma;* the most he can see through it is extremely bright light. He retains some peripheral vision–he estimates 45 degrees–with acuity measured at 20/400. Over time and with enough contact, he can generally figure out what another person looks like. With a special microscopic reading lens, he can read print but, he says, "a normal three or four paragraph letter can take me 25 minutes to read."

Lou was 35 before he experienced his first symptom of Meniere's Syndrome–intense vertigo. He dismissed the first attack as the consequence of eating some overripe food–bad clams, perhaps. Within the following year, the attacks increased in frequency. He also began to experience tinnitus–ringing and whirring noises in his right ear. He consulted physicians and ultimately received the diagnosis of Meniere's Syndrome and the prognosis of a hearing loss, at that point in only the right ear. His hearing, however, did not decline substantially until about 1974 when he was 44 years old. He has learned to control the vertigo; the tinnitus is frequently just a background hum of noise; and though he has a bilateral hearing loss classified as "severe," with additional losses at specific frequencies causing poor speech discrimination, he has acquired some powerful auditory aids that enable him to hear well in many situations.

Lou grew up in Rochester, New York, the youngest in a family of 10 children. His parents were Sicilian immigrants and he describes his old neighborhood as a "Sicilian ghetto." Affecting a righteous falsetto of authority, he says he had a "very bad high school record." He was a frequent truant, had poor grades, and was engaged in a certain amount of fraudulent activity ("hustling" and "rip-offs") that he describes as almost a cultural phenomenon—"do unto others before they do unto you." His major concerns were his image and reputation as a well-dressed, club-hopping playboy. He was "tossed out" of high school before completing the 10th grade. At 18, largely to escape his family, he joined the Army, serving for 3 years before his glaucoma was discovered and he was granted a medical discharge.

The discovery was in some ways accidental. Shortly before he was due to be discharged, he went to the post dispensary, hoping to have a free eye examination and, if he needed them, a free pair of glasses before returning to civilian life. Instead, he learned that with his eye condition, he should never have been in the Army, to which he replied, with typical dry humor, "Well, this is a helluva time to tell me. I've been in the Army 3 years." He was placed in a hospital, then sent home to New York. "I still had vision. I had lost some in my right eye, I was aware of that. But I still had very good vision in my left eye, 20/20 in my left eye. So I kind of went along with that. I have to admit, I was 21 years old, I had some livin' I wanted to do. I didn't want to be messin' around with any eye condition."

His parents had retired to Arizona and Lou's brothers ran the family business—a bakery. He joined as a full partner, but was, he says, "totally uninvested." "I just did my work and let my older brothers make all the decisions—just as long as I got my money at the end of the week." He was a jazz buff and as concerned with his image as he had been in high school. He went out almost every night—making the rounds of the nightclubs, dressed in expensive suits, seen with attractive women, known by the club owners and bartenders. He says, "There was also a marriage in there, by the way, when I was 25, which was a complete disaster and should never have occurred."

In 1953, Lou had three operations to control the pressure

in his right eye; the surgery destroyed his residual vision and left him with a very painful and scarred eye, but emotionally he was unable to "give it up" until 1956. By 1957 he developed the *scotoma* in the other eye and began to "really get in touch with the fact" that he was "starting to be in trouble with the left eye." Until he was declared legally blind in 1958–he had a "quirk" of being able to read eye charts, though little else–he spent 2 years as principal actor in a "comedy of errors trying to get help from vocational rehabilitation." Since he was not considered legally blind, he went to the general division of vocational rehabilitation (DVR) rather than to the state Services for the Blind.

In the late fifties, DVR sent Lou for 5 days of psychological evaluation–using paper and pencil tests that he could barely see. At that point, he says, "I was very uptight about the whole issue of my blindness. I wasn't copping to it at all." He did not make it clear that his eyesight was too poor for reading the tests. "On the fifth day, they may have given me the verbal section of the Wechsler Adult Intelligence Scale. By then, I didn't even know my own name. Then I had an appointment with the counselor at voc rehab. She wanted me to sit down, she wanted to talk to me. She said that while I was a very nice young man, I should understand that there were some very serious limitations on what I might be able to do. Apparently I had come out on the tests as a borderline defective."

"Now, even before I went back to school, I was a pretty articulate fella. I'd always read a lot. Interestingly enough, it was not my voc rehab counselor at all, but a woman at the state employment service who got the test results who said, 'This is total insanity. This does not fit at all with my concept of your capabilities.' She put up a big stink and said I was not being properly evaluated. Over a year passed before we got through all this, but she insisted that I be evaluated at a center for the blind."

In his subsequent evaluation, Lou "came out smelling like a rose." His IQ was established as 135, which, he says, "is not borderline defective." The evaluators recommended professional training. "Voc rehab kind of plugged into me right away when they found out I had an IQ of 135. People at DVR all of a sudden said, 'We'll send you to school.' Then Services for the Blind came in and said, *'We'll* send you to school.'

Everybody wants a winner. When they thought I was borderline defective, it was 'Go away, Sonny.' If that sounds like an expression of bitterness, I mean it. It really irritates the hell out of me. When I moved to Kansas later, still under the auspices of New York State, Kansas was trying to pick me up. Missouri wanted to pick me up when I went back to work. Everybody wants to latch on to a winner. It's the name of the game—'Wow! We've got a Ph.D. for a client!'—guaranteed success story. It hasn't quite been that way."

Lou had earned a high school equivalency diploma while in the Army. He nonetheless had difficulty entering the University of Rochester—not because of his blindness, but because of his poor grades in high school and his dropout status. Fortunately, the University had an evening program, attended mostly by employees of Xerox, Kodak, and other large area firms. Although the courses were taught by University of Rochester professors and covered identical curriculums as the day classes, the evening program had no entrance requirements. Lou studied at night for 2 years until, having proved himself, he was accepted as a transfer student in the undergraduate degree program.

Entering college, he was faced with note taking, reading, and studying. His vision was too poor for him to read print. He had Braille instruction for 1 year, but found it painstaking, difficult, and too time-consuming at a point when his course work demanded his attention. Instead of Braille, he depended on readers, some paid by Services for the Blind, some volunteers; a tape recorder; and his memory. (His hearing was still "dynamite" at the time.) He took notes as well as he could in class, then had someone, also paid by the state agency, decipher them and read them into his tape recorder. One reader read all of his textbooks to him and into the machine. Lou says, "In some ways I feel, okay, I did the work and all that, but God, she read everything for me. I wouldn't have known where to begin without her. My family didn't know how to handle my blindness. About all they could do was get on the bandwagon when I graduated and fill up the stadium." Lou had separated from his first wife before entering college. During his first 2 years of school, he lived with his oldest sister's family. When he moved out to have more "space" of his own, his mother, he says, "sent poison pen letters to all of my brothers and sisters—they had 'abandoned their poor, blind brother, their poor, blind, *baby brother*' who happened to be 31 years old at the time!"

With a B.A. in psychology, Lou applied to graduate programs in clinical psychology. Although his academic record was good, he was continually rejected. His advisor tried to force the graduate schools to put on paper *why* they would not accept Lou, but he had little success. Both he and Lou felt, with considerable anger, that the rejections were due to his blindness. He worked for about 6 months as the coordinator of volunteers for a manpower program—a volunteer position itself—and tried to find paid employment through Services for the Blind and other agencies. He tells the story, "I saw one counselor at the state employment service who said, 'Oh, yes, we can find you a job,' then proceeded to describe a position where you count out sheets of wrapping paper and fold them." "I said to her, trying to be as polite as I could, that I was hoping to find something a little more commensurate with my educational background. Her reaction was, 'Well, you *are* blind,' at which point I got up, gave her a little half bow, and said, 'Madame, not half as blind as you are,' and walked out. It was a gut response and about the only thing I could get out without punching her out, which is what I wanted to do. I also reported her to her supervisor."

Lou explains some interesting aspects of his adjustment to blindness and his feelings about it now. He describes his first reaction as denial, which in his case included silence in situations when he could not see what was happening (as in his testing for DVR); and a convincing recitation for physicians and rehabilitation workers of the dates and names of his ailments and operations, a bit of showmanship camouflaging how little he actually understood and how lost he felt. He says, though, "I think a certain amount of denial is very functional, certainly in the beginning. A person goes through different stages. If I weren't denying at the beginning, I would have been sucked under. So part of my denial kept me from succumbing . . . as opposed to coping with the disability." He believes, too, that knowing one will lose or is slowly losing a sense is not preparation for the time that the scope of the loss becomes apparent. "Then it's almost like, psychologically, the reaction to passing the critical threshold, when it becomes evident that there is a significant loss, is like sudden onset of the disability. It has been that way for me and I've had contact with others for whom it's been similar."

Although one might expect that Lou's earlier preoccupation with his playboy image would be a detriment when blindness made the image and the activities that supported it no longer viable, he feels that his earlier values also worked to his advantage. He says, "In a sense it was a loss, not being a smooth, skilled operator. Before that, what had been important to me was, 'Did I look cool?' You know, expensive suits, always be seen with a good-looking woman; be a sport; be known. Then with the blindness I was in a different bag. But I think what motivated me to pick up on going back to school was a lot of that pride–a whole kind of Sicilian, macho pride. I didn't want to be a guy who was gonna stand on the corner or be working in a sheltered workshop weaving baskets or stuff like that. That was a bit much for me."

"I had a lotta skills that I had acquired earlier and took into my disability as advantages. I've always been pretty adaptable. I got by when I was a kid having to survive a bunch of older siblings. I got by in the military. The image stuff had its advantage in terms of my maintaining poise and getting people to relax with me. I had already gotten past the point of playacting and had incorporated a lot of the smoothness as part of me.

"Blindness got me back to school and that got me in touch with the fact that not only did I like working with people, but I was good at it. And it was good for me to know that I was good at something. Even though I had this big image thing and it was established that I was a pretty good playboy, when it came to working, I never had established that I could do anything well. It was kind of nice to have an identification somewhat more constructive than being able to pick good Scotch and find a good tailor. That's a rather limited distinction. It was nice to get feedback that I was a reasonably bright guy and that I had a way with people."

After a full year out of school, Lou was accepted for graduate study at the University of Kansas. The University had a program in rehabilitation psychology–somatapsychology. Although he entered their clinical psychology program, through individual professors he developed an association with the rehabilitation concentration. He feels that the University's having the somatapsychology program—and a commitment to rehabilitative endeavors—was an asset in his acceptance. He compares his enrollment as a blind student at University of Kansas with benefits people now receive from Affirmative Action programs. He says, "I had the grades, but there was also quite a bit of competition. I don't know if they accepted me because I was blind, but they sure as hell didn't reject me because of it."

Moving to a new community made life easier for him. He says, "My family and friends in Rochester had difficulty dealing with me. What they saw was someone they'd known as sighted who lost his sight. All they could focus on were the losses. When I moved to Kansas, everybody was meeting me as a blind man. Their expectations were that I would be a lot less functional than I actually was. A lot of people don't understand legal blindness, residual vision, that sort of thing. I was learning how to use that effectively and was really learning how to use my ears. The irony of my later having a hearing loss was that the way I used my ears was just incredible. In a room full of people, I could identify people by name in conversations when more than one person was talking at once. I also had practically perfect pitch for music."

Nonetheless, he experienced prejudice from some members of the graduate school faculty, about whom he says, "Psychologists, psychologists who are supposed to know human behavior, supposed to understand that we have unlimited potential, given the right circumstances.... Coming out of the East, I kind of went into culture shock when I came to the Midwest. I didn't know how to communicate; people found me abrasive. I was always into a lot of fast banter. That's just the way I'd always functioned."

"One particular professor and I were walking down the hall one day, and he asked me, 'Hey, are you really serious about being in this program and trying to get a doctorate in psychology?' I thought he was putting me on, I really did. I mean, why else would I be there? But I just said, 'Oh, no, not really. Fact is, I was sitting around collecting disability and I was really getting bored to death. I figured there was something I could do with my time so I might as well go to school, but no, I'm not interested in this.' I thought he would take it just the way I said it to him, as a joke. He didn't. But the point is, the prejudice was there in advance.

"When I had been through the program and was ready to take my doctoral comps, they had this big faculty meeting deciding how I was going to take them. I had always used readers in my exams. My professors just said, 'Here, take the exam home, go to another room, do whatever you want to do,' allowing, in some cases, a little extra time, which was not out of the ordinary. It had already been established–Educational Testing Service provides readers and extra time for blind students taking the Graduate Record Exam. But when they had this meeting, this same professor said, 'Well, if he can't take the comps like everyone else, he shouldn't be a psychologist,' whereupon my primary advisor, who was my master's thesis advisor, dissertation advisor, coauthor on a publication, and now a good friend, went into a rage. I heard about this from another faculty member. He said, 'Where in the hell is he gonna find, in the outside world functioning as a psychologist, a situation as artificial as doctoral comps?' That put it to rest.

"I had my problems with prejudice in graduate school, but I had some pretty powerful people supporting me who had an investment in my getting a degree. I'm not saying they had an investment because they wanted to graduate a blind student; I think the investment was a personal one. These are people who, to this day, write letters of recommendation for me and write pretty glowing ones."

During his second year of graduate school, Lou had had his first attack of vertigo. "I was at the American Psychological Association convention in New York City, waiting for a friend in the lobby of the Waldorf-Astoria. Fortunately, I was standing next to a pay telephone, because that's all I had to hang on to. I had a very severe attack of vertigo at that point. It was crazy. I've had the kind of vertigo that comes with drinking bad booze and drinking too much of it–when you lie down and the room starts spinning. That's one kind."

"The kind I'm talking about, you feel like there's a physical force pitching you. There's a spinnning sensation, dizziness. You're trying to walk forward and it's like having a physical force pitch you back. It's awful. Some people will be sitting at a desk and then suddenly be thrust forward and bang their heads on the top. Some people walking along will be pitched over backwards. In addition to that—and it took me a long time to figure this out, by the way—without an adequate visual anchor, it's even worse. My peripheral vision was just not enough—all I could be in touch with was that my world was going upside down. I've found myself in some pretty weird situations: sitting at the top of some stairs, hanging onto the railing scared to death."

For about a year, Lou had several more, "terrible, terrible attacks" that lasted 4 or 5 hours, caused vomiting, and left him "wiped out for 72 hours afterward." At about the same time he began to notice the noise in his ears—"ringing, rushing, whirring, humming." He went to the university health clinic; they sent him to the University of Kansas Medical Center in Kansas City to see the otologist who diagnosed his problem as Meniere's Syndrome.

"When I got the diagnosis of Meniere's, I had the gross misfortune of having it done by a superb, an outstanding otologist who, as a person, is probably the worst son of a bitch who ever walked the face of the earth. I stood there and he said, 'Well, you have Meniere's Syndrome and blah, blah, blah, blah.' I said, 'Wait a minute. Can you back up? What can we do about this?' He said, 'Nothing.' I said, 'Can you give me anything in the way of relief?' He said, 'Sure, we can go in there and do surgery, basically gut out your inner ear. That will eliminate all the tenderness and it will also eliminate your hearing.' I said, 'Well, you know, can you give me anything... in between?' And he said, 'Look, you're a scientist. You should understand that research on this thing is very poor. We've tried different things and nothing is guaranteed to be any good. Some people think vitamins, some people think medication of one kind or another. None of this stuff has really been all that effective on a consistent basis.' I said, 'Well, what can we try to give me relief from some of this nausea—some Dramamine or something?' And he said, 'Dramamine, Marezine, Dizzy Dean, what the hell's the difference?' I looked at him and said, 'Hey, do you hear what I'm saying to you? I'm saying to you that I already have one sensory loss and you're telling me that I might have another one coming up, and that scares the hell out of me.' And he said, 'Well, there's nothing I can do for you,' and that was it. I just left. But I've changed since then. If that happened today, he would catch it. He would have a run for his money. He might throw me out of his office, but he would know that he got told off. It's that kind of insensitivity that's hard to take."

Lou was 35 years old when he received the diagnosis of Meniere's; he was still taking classes toward his doctorate. In one class as a professor was demonstrating clinical applications of hypnosis, Lou discovered that when his pulse rate was increased, an attack of vertigo followed. The reverse was also true. When the pulse rate was decreased, symptoms of an oncoming attack subsided. Working with the professor, Lou taught himself to control the attacks. He noticed that just before he became dizzy, his tinnitus would reach a higher pitch than usual. Using that variation as a cue, he learned to use self-hypnosis to relax himself sufficiently to avoid the vertigo.

By that time, his tinnitus was as it has remained, always present. Frequently–good days–it is just a background hum of noise. At other times he compares it to "a high frequency motor with an insistent whine, like a whirring sensation." "Sometimes it's like standing next to Niagara Falls with a massive generator going and a couple of sirens in the background. There's that much sound. When I'm feeling frazzled or overworked, it's really a bitch. When I say overworked, I mean cranking out too much energy. It takes a lot more energy for me to do what you can do more easily. That's not a 'poor me' stance–that's the name of the game. Then I feel like screaming, 'Please, I've got to have some *real* quiet!' "

For several years, Lou's hearing remained stable. He finished graduate school, married ("Marriage Number Two"), completed an internship, started a job, divorced, underwent open heart surgery, resumed his job, and was fired.

He had devised his own non-traditional internship at a Veterans' Administration center. Although he did the standard work on the hospital's psychiatric wards, he devoted most of his time to working with disabled individuals in the nursing home care unit. He also acted as consultant on the surgical floor, counseling on the psychological aspects of dealing with surgery, and conducted workshops on death and dying. He was offered a position as unit psychologist of the spinal cord injury unit of a Veterans' Administration hospital in California, but a series of events at the hospital upset his plans to actually work there. The position had previously been offered to a psychologist already on the hospital staff. When that man refused it, the personnel administrator promised, "If ever you change your mind . . . ." The man changed his mind, and the offer to Lou was rescinded.

At the time the job fell through, Lou was going through "Separation Number Two." He is not talkative about his marriages—in fact, he mentioned the third one only as an afterthought. He says he does not believe his disabilities were factors in the dissolution of any of them; instead, he feels each time he and his spouse married for the wrong reasons. He remains "terrific" friends with his second wife. But with the second marriage "going down the tube," his disappointment about the job in California, and increasing signs—and fears—of the hearing loss, Lou did not feel stable enough to leave the area where he had lived for more than 5 years. He declined a position in Cleveland, opting instead to stay where he had a support group of friends.

Shortly afterward, he moved from Lawrence, Kansas (where the university was located) to Kansas City, Missouri to work as staff psychologist in a diagnostic and rehabilitation unit of the county jail. When that program ended, he worked in the Criminal Justice System's drug treatment program, first as director of the diagnostic unit, then as director of the outpatient treatment center. He enjoyed the work, the responsibility that accompanied it, the salary, and the benefits that he earned, but for reasons that he prefers not to have published, he resigned.

Leaving the job in 1975, he discovered the severity of his hearing loss. He realized that while he had been "the boss," his staff had accommodated him without his knowing it. Suddenly, he had to do the adjusting for communication. He was also rapidly losing more of his hearing. Emotionally, the loss had a far more profound impact than that of his blindness 20 years before.

"The hearing loss is a freak-out. It just kind of blew me away originally. I thought, well, I don't mind telling you I was seriously contemplating suicide. When it became evident that I was losing my hearing significantly, I thought, 'That's it. I just can't tolerate the isolation that goes with the blindness compounded with the hearing loss.'

"When I lost my sight, I lost the ability to do things; I lost the ability to drive. I could still go to clubs and parties and be charming and witty and all that, but it was harder. But, as I said, I also learned that I could do other things. But when I started to lose my hearing, I thought, 'Uh-uh, now we're going a little too far. We're starting to push the limits.'

"The deafness taught me one thing, and it's still kind of a bitter lesson. I learned to discard a lot of people with my deafness. The situation now is that people who want to communicate with me have to put out some effort themselves. I can't do it all myself. And it can be damned hard work to communicate with me. I've had to find out who the people are who are willing to crank out all the energy it takes, to do it over time, not just in one-to-one situations, and to put up with all the crap it takes when we go out for dinner together. I never lost people with my sight loss."

The added disability paralyzed Lou for a time—in fact, for a couple of years. Since losing the job with the prison, he has been unable to find another full-time position. As with his divorces, he is loath to blame his problems on his disabilities. He acknowledges that Kansas City's glutted market for psychologists and his ambivalence about moving away, particularly to an isolated area, have contributed to his difficulty in finding the kind of work he would like. But he believes the dual disability, and his reaction to the hearing loss, have compounded the problem. In some cases, he says, to find a staff position or to build a private practice in psychotherapy, one must be visible and well-known. Until recently, Lou has been uncomfortable enough with his hearing loss to put his energy into being *invisible*. Although he maintained social relationships, he did not involve himself in community affairs; he also restricted his professional activities.

About 1½ years after losing his job, however, he did find a steady part-time position as a consultant counseling clergy in career development. He has also maintained several private clients, with some of whom he barters services; he offers counseling in exchange for their reading his mail to him or cleaning his apartment. In exchange for research and typing, he has also supervised one psychologist needing to accumulate hours of supervised clinical experience. After several years of limited activity, Lou has begun to involve himself in community programs with the goal of becoming more visible. Among his activities is leading workshops on death and dying at the local Free University.

Lou has also joined a task force evaluating services for disabled individuals in several Kansas and Missouri counties. The group has found that comprehensive services are not available in rural areas and that information about existing programs is not provided to people who need it. Many physicians and hospitals do not appropriately refer prospective clients. Other task force recommendations of particular interest to Lou concern the acquisition of mechanical devices, the attitudes of professionals who work with disabled individuals, and the Social Security system.

Lou spent 9 months waiting for the auditory trainer he uses for amplification. It is a powerful FM transmitter-receiver system. Although he has several other auditory aids, including standard hearing aids, it is the auditory trainer unit that he credits with "getting me back into the world" after the hearing loss. In addition to supplying amplification, it is sensitive only to those sounds near the transmitter microphone, thus filtering out the background noise that an ordinary hearing aid increases for him. It also acts as a "compressor," reducing high volume noises to a level Lou, who is sensitive to loud sounds, can tolerate.

Lou believes he received the unit through Services for the Blind after 6 months only because he suggested he might contact his state representative about the time required for the delivery of equipment essential to his functioning. In his area, some agencies order such equipment along with pencils and paper. Lou will recommend that it get separate, priority handling. He believes he could also benefit from a closed-circuit TV magnifying system, through which printed material held under a TV camera appears magnified on a screen. The agency serving him, however, does not consider it essential to his functioning and he cannot afford the $1,000 it costs.

Lou feels strongly that many–although he stresses certainly not all–rehabilitation workers and medical professionals treat clients with condescension and paternalism.

He says, "Some counselors act like they're paying for equipment themselves. Not only are they not paying for it, the agency isn't paying for it. In my case, because I get Social Security benefits, they're reimbursed by the Federal Government. That's the kind of thing that irritates me. Also, a lot of programs don't take into account individual variability and an individual's needs. They don't consider the stage of adjustment a person is at. Then I've had counselors talk to me like I'm an idiot and as if to say, 'Squirm, you bastard.' And that's not just my impression. I had a friend with me when one counselor rolled her eyes and did the whole condescension bit when I asked for information."

He believes the rehabilitation system is paradoxical in fostering such behavior. "On the one hand they tell you to 'rehabilitate yourself,' but then they say, 'you have to jump through the hoop when we tell you.' I would like to see some real educating of some of those people and some very specific demands: that part of their job is to remember they're civil servants and treat people like human beings. I've been a consumer *and* a provider of services and, damn it, one thing I've always felt is extremely important is to respect clients as human beings."

Since earning his doctorate, Lou has been able to avoid negative attitudes of professionals he encounters, for, as he says, "I got myself a title." He has contacts that lead him to better services. His first audiologist suggested he use an ear trumpet, basically a large tube that, when placed with one end at the speaker's lips and the other at the hard-of-hearing person's ears, channels sound directly to the hearing impaired person in a system only slightly more sophisticated than simple cupping of the ear. Through a friend, though, he was referred to his present audiologist. He says, "Now my audiologist is not only my audiologist, he's a good friend of mine. With a lot of other people I push the 'Dr.' in front of my name and I get preferred treatment. I don't like doing it, but it's a reality. I'm not knocking it for myself, but I think it's too bad that other people can't get that treatment . . . and a little dignity." Lou says he has experienced so much condescension while traveling that now, although he won't permit clients to call him Dr. Cordaro, he always uses his title when making reservations.

Social Security has presented Lou the same conundrum it

offers many other disabled individuals. He feels it is a system with no incentive for people to work. After he lost his job, he received sizable payments from Social Security, although no one could tell him how they were computed. There was a limit, however, to what he could earn above his benefits. Those restraints would make it impossible for him to work enough to advance in his field, and as he says, "I am 48 years old." Now that he has gone off Social Security, he has to pay all of his own health insurance and Social Security tax on his income 3 percent higher than that paid by an individual whose company contributes. He is actually making less money now than he could on Social Security. He says, though, "I want to be in the world."

There are events and relationships, however, from which Lou is excluded, and from which he may always be excluded. He is open about his reactions to the limiting aspects of his disabilities: "In a lot of ways, I have a zest for life and I feel like I'm being deprived–having to depend on these goddamned machines, and having to depend on other people, and on every other goddamned thing that isn't *me*."

"Last night I gave a workshop on death and dying and one woman was getting angry, but what she was saying, really saying was 'Go away-closer,'–get the hell away from me, but please don't go. I shared with her some of my feelings around my sense of loss over losing my sight and hearing. You know, my eyes died and my ears died, and in a sense, it was the death of a phase and a way of being; having to be another way, and not by choice. That's what makes me so mad sometimes, that I don't have any choice. So I get angry, I get hurt, and sometimes I just say, 'Poor me.' I get furious if anybody else pities me, but sometimes I want to be able to pity myself.

"I feel anguish. Sometimes I feel really cheated. I lost my sight and broke my back going to school and getting a Ph.D. and then just working a couple of years and wham, having to deal with all this crap with the hearing loss. I have screamed, hollered, cried, and when I'm saying it now I can feel an ache in my gut and a tightening in my throat, and if I went with this now, the tears would just start welling up. I'm angry as hell. I feel fucked. I'd be lying to you if I said that I put to rest the issue of suicide, of taking my own life. If

I got worse, I don't know what I'd do. It's like the tinnitus—suicide is there every day, but sometimes it's noticeable and sometimes it's in the background. I've had a colleague come to consult with me about a client—about suicide as an alternative. I asked him, 'Why me?,' and he said because he thinks I must deal with it all the time. Very perceptive.

"I'm not gonna run around like a Pollyanna. I'm acutely aware of what I've lost. I used to get such enjoyment out of music; now most music sounds cacophonous to me. I used to read anything; now I have to get things recorded and do the selective process. I would give anything to sit down and browse through my books or jump in a car and drive out to the country by myself and go as far as I want to go and stop where I want to stop.

"On one level, though, I feel lucky. Because of my commitment to my profession and how I work in my profession, I also have a commitment to living that way—to getting those emotions out. I have literally felt myself going over the edge with anguish and despair, but I've had someone just hanging in there with me and saying, 'Go ahead, it's what you need.' It's been painful. I'm grieving and I may be grieving all my life. I'll probably always be angry. But part of what keeps me going is my anger."

Lou believes that his friendships are not accidents. He knows that he can ask for support from his friends, but they know, too, that he will reciprocate. Support includes not only emotional nurture at critical times, but such things as rides as well. He has "contracted" with his friends—he asks them directly for a ride when he needs it and repays them when he can with some other service. Friends sometimes respond to his requests with, "No, I can't," or "No, I don't feel like it." He says a refusal may make him angry, but his relationships are more honest than those in which the disabled individual is treated gingerly. He has experienced the delicate treatment from other acquaintances; he says, "Sometimes I wish people would show me the courtesy of getting mad at me."

More complicated relationships are those with members of his family. Although he seems to understand the dynamics in that area, he does not explain them as articulately as he does other topics. Some factors in the tense relationships, he feels, are not connected with the disabilities. He had always been the maverick in the family—the "marginal bum." He was also the "baby," raised more by his oldest siblings than by his parents. With his education and experience–when he earned his doctorate, he was the only one of his siblings who had graduated from college–his value system and worldview are not altogether consonant with those of his family; for one thing, he is not interested in getting involved with family feuds and factions in Rochester.

But he thinks, too, that part of the problem is directly related to the disabilities and to his Sicilian background. In the culture he was reared in, men did not show sensitive emotions–crying might be permissible, but only in rage. Part of that ethic holds that a disability, particularly in a male, is an inadequacy, and he feels his family has communicated that message without realizing it. He remembers in college approaching a brother and saying, "I don't know if I can handle all this," and his brother's giving him a peptalk–"You're doing great. There are people worse off than you." Lou says, "I knew there were people worse off than me. I just wanted somebody to hear I was hurting."

During his first visit to Rochester after losing his hearing, he and his sister were "practically at each other's throats." But he attributes that to his own behavior and to his family's caring. He suspects that it is painful for them to see him struggling and therefore they prefer not to deal with his disabilities openly. Similarly he remembers his own anguish in not being able to comfort his sister during a Christmas visit when she had been recently widowed, and his feeling of absurdity that although he is a trained professional who works with people in grief, he could not help someone in his family whom he loves. He has since had a job interview in Rochester and arranged his schedule to celebrate that sister's 70th birthday with her. He felt this time that communication was easier and relationships were less strained–and he says one reason for the improvement is his own changing attitude. Although he has lost more hearing, he has learned to trust more what he does hear; he has also learned to ask for help more gracefully, and not to be so overwhelmingly effusive in his thanks. As he becomes more comfortable with the disabilities, he relates to his family with greater ease.

Accepting the disabilities is an on-going process for Lou. In graduate school he became enraged when a companion remarked on how well he maneuvered in the cafeteria. He said to her, "You're not impressed with my ability as a blind man, you're impressed with my ability as an actor–to act as if I'm not blind." With his hearing loss, he found "subtle, manipulative ways of resisting, avoiding situations where I have to say I'm disabled." Entering a restaurant with a friend, he would drop back to have the other person request a small table in a quiet corner. But with a few years' adjustment he can more frequently say, "I have to do this myself this time," and ask for what he needs.

But he says, "I can look like Mr. Adjustment himself and I do to a lot of people. I'm not. I'm still fighting. I'm kicking and screaming all the way. The difference between sitting here and telling you I'm blind and being out there on the street carrying a cane is like the difference between saying you're a great liberal and having to put it on the line by carrying a sign around the courthouse."

Lou does, however, always take a folded cane with him when outdoors, using it at intersections and in other situations when he feels it is necessary. He uses it, too, as identification that he is "someone in need of special considerations" and he feels that all legally blind people should do likewise. When he became more comfortable acknowledging the hearing loss, he wore his hair shorter for awhile to make the hearing aids obvious, but he says it did not work; people do not notice. He says, "Some people are very impressed that I don't look disabled, but it creates problems for me. I wish sometimes my disabilities were more identifiable. Instead I have to clearly establish my needs for people. I have to say, 'I'm disabled, will you accommodate me in this way?' It's tough."

Lou has had some encounters with those whom he calls "super helpers" who drag him across the street. He says, "I try to convey to people, 'Let me set the parameters.' People whom I deal with on a continued basis know that." Aware of his varying needs of denial, assertion, experimentation, self-sufficiency, he says, "I can be walking with one of my friends when it's pitch black. If I don't grab that person's arm, it's my tough luck. It's not that they won't hang back for me to grab it. But if I don't take it, it's my problem, not theirs."

"You know, all the heavy stuff with the disabilities is back there for me. I just don't walk around obsessing about the crap I deal with because of them. I don't have time to do that, just from a standpoint of what I'm trying to do to establish myself professionally at this point. Sometimes it gets me sucked under, but more often than not, it's just back there. You can't make the disabilities go away. It's living with a daily annoyance and quite often you ignore it. Psychologically, I wouldn't advise what I've been doing right now—going back and focusing on the losses. I've come a long way and I do feel that the disabilities have contributed positively to my really assessing my life and seeing where I am and what my values are. I do have disabilities and, yes, my disabilities are a part of me, but they certainly are not the totality of who I am as a person. I function as a person far beyond the limitations of my disabilities. I've lost a lot of control over my life in a lot of ways, but I've had to exercise a lot of control in making determinations of how I can live it within the circumstances that occur. Recently I've been able to say, 'Hey, I'm having a good day today,' rather than saying, 'I may be having a good day, but it's not the way it was.'

"If you're familiar with the rehab literature, maybe you know the name Beatrice Wright. Beatrice is a professor at K.U. and a good friend. Last time I talked with her, I was talking about my needs and how I've been able to become more assertive around specifying them. She said to me, 'Lou, would you entertain a different word from *aggressive* or *assertive*?' I said, 'Sure, you know, out with it.' And she said, 'I feel like when you specify your needs, you *affirm* yourself. It's an *affirming* statement.' *Affirmation* is a much better word than *assertion* because it's saying, yes, I'm making a clear declaration of where I am. It's not a bulldozing thing; it's an affirmation of myself, and that's a very positive thing."

Joan Tiller*

Joan Tiller infuriates professional rehabilitation counselors in her community, for she refuses (she would say *declines*) to use a white cane or assert her communication needs in meetings, and prefers not to talk about any emotional effects of her disabilities. Those counselors who know Joan socially–she does not consult any as a client–like her and think she is intelligent and in command of her life. They feel, too, that she denies her disabilities, thereby making certain situations more difficult and even dangerous for herself. If, for some people, living with a disability means balancing on a fine line between denial and acceptance–knowing that acceptance may lead to submission–then Joan may be at that line.

Joan's vision and hearing impairments fit into no neat classifications. When she was 4 years old, she poked her right eye with a fork, damaging the cornea. She retained some vision in the eye, but it no longer functioned properly in coordination with her left eye. She says that she does not know what depth perception is. The right eye was surgically removed when she was 25 and replaced with a plastic prosthesis.

When she was 8 years old, she developed conical cornea in her left eye, a condition in which the normally spherical outer layer of the eye is cone shaped, preventing the eye from refracting light properly. For a few years, deposits of

---

*Names of people and places have been changed, including cities and states.

"bubbles and film" on the cornea blocked her pupil; she says, "When I was 8 to 10 years old, my sight was about what you'd see looking through a frosty bathroom window." The obstruction on the cornea began to move sideways when she was a teenager, an unusual occurrence, and by the time she was 15 her vision had improved significantly.

Joan's vision problem may also be related to Marfan's Syndrome, a congenital hereditary condition characterized by a partial dislocation of the crystalline lens in the eye's interior, miosis (very small pupils), and arachnodactyly (extremely long, thin bones), and sometimes associated with hearing loss. Joan has the small pupils, bone structure, and hearing loss associated with the syndrome, but her eye problems are not typical.

According to optometric testing, her vision has remained stable for the past 20 years, and is measured as 20/100 with the best corrective lenses. (Joan must be 20 feet from an object to see what a normally-sighted person sees at a distance of 100 feet.) Since her acuity is better than 20/200 and her peripheral vision includes more than 20 degrees, she is not legally blind. However, her eyes are "dazzled" by light. She explains, "Severe stigmatism tends to scatter bright light I see. Under some conditions, I would see a smirch of light where you see a point." If cars without their headlights on approach from the direction of the sun in the early morning or at dusk, she may not see them. Her eyes also adjust slowly to changes in light intensity. Entering a dimly-lit restaurant, she may not see for a full minute; seated across from other people, she will not see their faces if a candle is in front of them or another light source is behind them.

Her hearing loss is sensorineural (nerve deafness), a deterioration of some part of the intricate inner ear. Her loss is similar to the decline that many people experience as they age. In Joan's case, the loss became problematic when she was still a teenager. (Before that, she may have had a hearing loss, for she recalls having speech therapy as a child, training her to say church and squirrel correctly. She says, "I never heard the *ch* and *sc* sounds, which is the first sign of deafness in some people.") Her hearing has declined slowly but steadily since she was 15. She lost all of the hearing in her left ear after a bout with the flu several years ago. The loss in her right ear is measured at 95 decibels, improvable with a hearing aid. At this point, however, aids often distort speech sounds for her as much as they amplify them. As she says about using the telephone, "I can hear the voices, I can sometimes tell who is talking, I can tell that the person is becoming frustrated, but I can't tell what he's saying."

Joan is now 37 years old and single. She is nice looking and difficult to place in an age category; she seems to fit in well with people both older and younger than herself. She grew up in New York attending a state residential school for the blind and graduating from a small state college with a B.A. degree in sociology. She worked for 8 years as a writer and editor for the public affairs office of a scientific research institute near New York City. When her father, who also worked at the institute as an administrative scientist, retired and her parents moved to Lorwood, Washington, a small town in the mountains about an hour's drive from Seattle, she accompanied them.

She works for an advisory group to Seattle's mayor on programs related to handicapped individuals. In her position as communications coordinator (a title that she jokingly acknowledges is ironic, for communication is the area in which she most feels the effects of her disabilities), she has set up a telecommunication message relay system to enable the county's hearing impaired citizens to alert fire and police departments and ambulance services of emergency situations in their homes. She is also working on a relay system for nonemergency telephone messages (doctors' appointments, long distance personal calls), a telecommunication weather and news service, and more captioned programs on local TV stations. She prepares the advisory group's newsletter for interested organizations of and for disabled individuals and works on grant proposals and an assortment of other projects.

Joan began her education in a regular public school classroom but transferred to a special class for blind children, where she started to learn Braille, after her left eye developed the cornea problem. The school's program allowed the disabled children to spend parts of the school day in a regular classroom. By the time Joan was in the sixth grade, the film on her cornea had begun to move to the side of her eye, allowing her to see rather well for academic situations; she was able to spend most of her school day in the regular classroom.

She entered a state school for the blind, however, in the seventh grade, and stayed through high school. She explains, "By the time I graduated, I could read standard print; but when I started, my sight was still fairly bad. There really was not much mainstreaming. They just didn't do that. My parents could have tried something different, but they would really have had to make a big fuss to put me in a regular school. A lot of the local schools were very big, and with the handicap, I may have needed a smaller environment."

Joan supports mainstreaming disabled children in regular classrooms provided there is a great deal of support from both the child's family and the school, including not only readers for blind students and interpreters for deaf students, but also a commitment to the child's social and emotional growth. She believes that flexibility of programming is necessary for both mainstreamed situations and special classes. Her younger brother, Dan, also has a hearing loss, and though his is not so severe as hers, it showed up earlier. He spent 2 or 3 years in a special class "that consisted of Dan, another kid with a slight hearing problem, a couple of kids with perception problems, and a couple of behavioral problems. Guess what the teacher did all day. She disciplined the behavior problems. My mother considers those years a complete waste. Dan said he felt like a pariah; they didn't even have recess with the other kids. And normal children can be cruel sometimes if you're different."

Joan does not regret that she attended the school for the blind, although she feels that some of the other students may have resented her because she could see. She feels, though, that it was altogether a positive experience and, because of several excellent teachers, her education was challenging. The school's superintendent at the time, however, tended toward an attitude of overprotection or limited expectations of his students.

"In any boarding school, you are somewhat restricted in what normal teenagers consider normal things to do ... like dating without having to listen to long lectures about how two blind people should never get married. Every time the superintendent thought there was a couple getting too serious, he would call all the girls together and give his lecture. He didn't want any 'lolligagging in the cupola'–the archways of the school. I think part of his concern was the heredity. If he had gone about it differently, I think the students may have listened to him, because they were concerned about it too. They didn't want to have children who had our problem. But he just got to be such a joke.

"There was a blind lawyer. He had gone to Perkins or one of those schools when our superintendent was in charge there. He was totally blind and, I think, had practiced before the Supreme Court of Connecticut. When I was at my school, the man was featured on the television program 'This Is Your Life.' Our superintendent was game enough to go on as the superintendent who had told him he should never go to college. I didn't hear the whole thing because everybody gathered around the TV was laughing so hard. But that was this man's attitude and he carried it from school to school."

Joan's main complaint with the school is that she had trouble getting into college. "They weren't encouraging students to go. But if you were college potential, they would send you to a regular high school in the morning. At that time, you had no chance of getting into college with only the school for the blind diploma by itself. I think now some of the better students are going full time to the public high school and getting support services from the state school."

"My problem was that by the time I started that, at the age of 15, my hearing had started to go down, and neither the school for the blind nor the public high school was really equipped to deal with someone with the dual handicap. At first, the hearing loss sneaks up on you and you don't believe it's really happening. Singing off key and not really sure why. I thought I was on key–but nobody else did. For awhile it was more of an annoyance than anything else. I couldn't sing in the school choir any more or be in the school plays–I couldn't hear my cues. It became frustrating. It got increasingly difficult to hear in class. But then I'd get a better hearing aid and I'd be back in business again. That went on for a long time. The hearing kept going down and the hearing aids kept getting stronger–so I kind of stayed about the same."

Joan has been using hearing aids for 20 years and has

dissatisfactions with the common method of their distribution. As a teenager she went to a hearing aid dealer for a hearing test and aid fitting. The aid she received was too strong and she believes it may have further damaged her hearing. She feels there should be more official regulation of hearing aid dealers. With the present system, most dealers carry only a limited number of brands, thus restricting a client's opportunity to find equipment well-matched to the particular variation of pitch and decibel loss he experiences. Since her first incorrect fitting, she has chosen aids through audiologists qualified to determine her amplification needs, then has purchased the devices from dealers the audiologists have recommended.

When Joan was a teenager and attending the public school part-time, she had one poor mathematics teacher who had difficulty making trigonometry comprehensible to her students. This teacher also spent part of the classroom time espousing her beliefs that blind students, in addition to not attending college, should not even bother with high school mathematics. The school for the blind was looking for an advanced level mathematics teacher at the time—the position requires both a background in the subject and knowledge of the special Braille symbols. Joan's father helped her when she went home on weekends, but with the poor teaching, her hearing loss preventing her from understanding lectures, and her limited vision making it difficult to see the blackboard, she missed too much material to receive a solid background for the college work in the sciences that she would have liked to pursue.

Dating is the only other area in which Joan feels she might have been hampered by her disabilities as she grew up—although, as with the mathematics, she is reluctant to attribute her experiences directly to them. She says, "A limited social life is probably unavoidable in any school with a small population. There were eight kids in my graduating class. The kids who didn't want to go to college tended more to date. Only one of the boys in my class was going to college. I didn't date much because I didn't have that much in common with anyone. I was also very studious, and I was reading a lot to make up for what I didn't hear in class. But which comes first? You tend to be more studious because you can't do the other, and it's a vicious circle sometimes." Joan says, too, that she has always been rather quiet and shy, and that having a hearing loss and being shy can be another vicious circle.

After graduating—from both the school for the blind and the public high school—Joan went to a state college. She chose sociology as a major because with her hearing loss and her problems with mathematics she thought it would be futile to major in a science. "I might have become a scientist if I could either see or hear better, but in chemistry, I couldn't see the results of some of the experiments and in lectures, I couldn't hear everything. If I had been deaf, I might have gone to Gallaudet and gone on with the sciences. But I chose sociology because it was easier for me and also because I wanted to help people."

For the first 2 years, she did well sitting in the front of her classrooms. An interpreter would not have helped for she knew no sign language. She feels that if she had had enough vision to supplement her hearing with lipreading, she would not have had much of a problem, for by periodically replacing her hearing aids, she was able to keep her hearing at a usable level. She also copied other people's notes. "Most people were cooperative. I'd pay them back at exam time. I was the only person who had complete notes—they were from about three different people."

Joan did not feel like an outcast during college. She did not date much, but says, "I was a very studious person. I was always up in the library studying with the canteen. I had close friends. I had the same roommate all through college." She describes the frustrations she did experience socially as "what most deaf people feel—having to convince people I was not *stupid*, I just couldn't hear what they were *saying*." "Sometimes students who didn't know me well would come up to me and say, 'Oh, I found out you're such a nice person. I called to you in the hall and you just kept walking. I thought you were stuck up.' That always left me feeling 'How many other people are there who haven't come, sat down, and talked?' " Although when someone did make an effort to be friendly with her, Joan would sit down and explain her hearing loss, she says, "When you're neither one nor the other (neither deaf nor fully hearing), it's hard for people to understand. When I was explaining, sitting in a quiet room side by side, I *could* hear; it's hard for someone to understand how it's different in a noisy cafeteria."

When she was a junior in college, her hearing took, as she says, a "nosedive." For the first time, a more powerful hearing aid did not help substantially. Schoolwork became more difficult and she started to have doubts that she would be able to go on to graduate school, a prerequisite for working in the field of sociology. She says she was frustrated and had dreams about committing suicide, although she believes that the dreams may also have come from another source, for the brother of a friend had recently killed himself. She was depressed, but she says, "I got disgusted with myself and went back to work–do something practical to get around it. I would get mad, get frustrated, but then I'd deliberately do something else to push it out of the way."

Two years later when she graduated from college, she was truly at a low point. "I saw I wasn't going to do what I had planned to do. My hearing was bad enough that I couldn't imagine coping with graduate school. I was tired. I had gotten good grades, but I was working too hard at it. I thought I had wanted to work with children. By the time I graduated, I couldn't even hear children."

Her right eye was a problem by then. It was painful and caused double vision. Because it was clouded over like an eye with glaucoma, its unattractiveness bothered other people. Her physician had been postponing its removal, for research on surgical restoration of the cornea was advancing rapidly. But that year, the doctor advised her to have it removed. Joan was basically relieved to get rid of it, but the recuperation period was somewhat traumatic. "For awhile I didn't want to be seen. You have a big hole in your head and a patch over the eye. Then they gave me a glass eye that didn't look like an eye at first. It really bothers people sometimes, and I was tired of people's reactions."

She spent about a year at home, unable to find a job, before she started working at the research institute. She looked for jobs for awhile, but found it difficult to garner the necessary enthusiasm. As she says, "Nobody wants to go to a job interview when they have a false thing in there. It was just glass, and evidently it would glint at people–my robot eye. I wasn't doing much that year. I was sitting at home.

That's when you end up pitying yourself. But it doesn't get you anywhere. You get up to here with pitying yourself and you want to do something about it . . . or a job comes along."

Joan worked at the research institute from 1966 to 1974. Her vision remained stable, as it had been all through college, but her hearing continued to decline. Most of the time a new hearing aid would help but, with the cumulative effects, she could never really recover what she lost. For 6 or 7 years she was able to hear well enough to interview people for an in-house newspaper for research institute employees, and she could still use the telephone. She lived in a suburb with her parents because, for most of the years that she was working, public transportation to the institute was not available.

While Joan was working at the institute, its computer center began to employ students from a nearby school for the deaf in a work-study program. The institute offered sign language classes for employees who had contact with the students, and Joan took advantage of that opportunity. She learned enough basic sign language to feel that as her hearing declined further, she would be able to build on what she knew. During her last year in New York, her hearing again dropped dramatically, another "nosedive," and Joan found herself unable to use the phone or to interview without "invading people's personal space."

"I had a choice then between staying in New York by myself, not knowing what direction my hearing was going in, or coming to Washington with my parents." She moved and found herself, for a second time, depressed and "inert." As when she was 25 and just out of college, the hearing loss seems to have precipitated her feelings; however, Joan is careful to point out that there were other factors, some perhaps secondary, some independent, that also contributed to her sense of hopelessness. For awhile she was living in Lorwood, "not the best place to initiate a job hunt." In addition, her mother did not really want her to go searching, and Joan says that that attitude frustrated her more than anything else.

She moved to an apartment in Seattle with her brother in order to search more actively. She applied to state vocational rehabilitation and was assigned a counselor with the services for the visually impaired who began to investigate employment possibilities for her. At the same time she followed likely leads to make her own contacts for herself. She says, "I was literally searching the newspaper, looking for names of people to write to." When a letter to the editor appeared from a volunteer with a local social and recreational organization for the six or eight identified deaf-blind people in Seattle, she dropped by to visit the woman who wrote the letter. An article describing new social work services for the deaf mentioned the name of the person heading that program, and Joan sent her a letter. She also made contact with the regional representative from the Helen Keller National Center for Deaf-Blind Youths and Adults.

Despite her efforts, she was unemployed for 18 months. During the first 6 months her hearing loss stabilized. She also found a hearing aid that amplified the low tones she had recently lost, and found she had to teach herself to identify the sounds that she had forgotten during the time they were inaudible, a process she has undertaken each time she has received a new aid. She did some hand weaving, a hobby at which she is accomplished, producing beautiful and intricately patterned wall hangings and bedcovers. She taught weaving to a deaf-blind woman in a nursing home, volunteer work which included researching methods of encoding weaving patterns in Braille, relearning Braille herself, transcribing the patterns, and helping to set up the looms. She also began a research project on P.P. Coleman, a Washington railroad pioneer who was her great-grandfather. While she found the research interesting, she did it also to "keep from climbing the walls." At the point when she was close to giving up on finding a job, her contact with people involved in services for the deaf and deaf-blind paid off. When the Comprehensive Employment and Training Act (CETA) program granted initial funding for the mayor's advisory group, the group's director asked the three women whom Joan had previously contacted for recommendations; he needed someone to start a newsletter for Washington's disabled population. They each suggested Joan, and ultimately she was offered the job. It turned out to be somewhat different from what was originally planned, but Joan has found her present work satisfying. She says, "I'm doing what I wanted to do–help people. I'm trying to build up some of the support systems that will help other people and will also help me."

Joan has been working in Seattle for a year-and-a-half. A year before assuming her job, she moved out of the temporary quarters with her brother, who moved to another part of the state. She is living now as a boarder in a private home, but the situation is more attractive than the term implies. She lives in a spacious house near a university; it is owned by a couple in their sixties who also rents rooms to two young men who are medical students. The couple travels frequently, and the whole house is frequently left to the boarders.

Joan has considered living alone, but she is ambivalent about the idea. First, she is too busy to find the time to go out and look for an apartment. Also, it is a task that would be easier to do with someone who could drive her around. She would like to have the space to bring all of her weaving looms together (her largest one is with her parents in Lorwood, whom she visits several weekends a month) in order to feel more permanently settled. At the same time, though, she is not sure that the advantages of living alone would compensate for the benefits she has now in sharing a house with other people.

Last year, Joan fell and tore her Achilles' tendon. The accident happened near her home and when the severity of the damage to her foot became apparent, her landlady brought her to the hospital for emergency care, and her roommates notified her parents via telephone. She supposes that if she lived alone in an apartment and had a serious accident, even with her Manual Communications Module (a portable telecommunication device), she might spend hours on the floor before she were able to reach another person with compatible equipment. Her roommates are cooperative in relaying phone messages between Joan and her parents and calling taxicabs for her when she must go out in the evening and does not have a ride. She feels, "Independent living for the handicapped can turn out to be very lonely. They end up in an apartment by themselves, a little less able to get out and contact people. I suppose that some people have found it's not all that it's cracked up to be."

Joan is involved with several organizations related to disabled people. As part of her job, she wrote a grant proposal for an experimental arts and wilderness program designed to bring together artists and severely disabled people to explore film making, photography, music, poetry, and other art forms. She has continued her involvement with the group, participating in their weekend-day trips and retreats to the mountains, and is secretary of the board of directors. She also tries to make contact and stay involved with organizations of deaf and deaf-blind individuals and with professionals who work with them. She generally participates in the monthly activities of the social group for deaf-blind individuals and has been attending the organizational meetings of Seattle's fledgling amateur theater of the deaf.

In addition to enjoying the social activities, she participates to strengthen her relationships with the other people involved. The funding that pays her present salary may be discontinued. Should the advisory group be unable to find another source of support, Joan may again be out of a job. She could probably continue to receive the disability annuity that she now collects as long as her income does not exceed 80 percent of her former earnings in New York. (She is considered "totally disabled" for performing the duties of her old job, for she cannot do the interviewing and telephoning that it required. In another sense, she is "rehabilitated," for she has other employable skills. She is not sure exactly where she stands with the annuity, and plans to check the regulations.) The annuity, however, gives her only $300 a month. She could try to live off the sale of her weaving, but the materials cost more than the prices people are willing to pay for the finished products. She cannot imagine herself becoming dependent on her parents at this point in her life. But even if she could keep afloat financially, she would not be doing the productive work that is important to her.

Yet Joan is not so uneasy with the prospect of having to find a new job as she has been in the past. She feels that her contacts, both work-related and social, with professionals serving the deaf and deaf-blind in Seattle will help her. Should she lose the rest of her hearing–and judging from past experience, she imagines she will–Joan intends to seek the aid of the other deaf-blind people whom she knows. She is sure that they will help her with the communication skills-more fluent comprehension of signs and tactile signing-that she will need to "get my feet back on the ground."

Communication remains Joan's biggest problem. She feels that she gets around well enough with buses and cabs, although it can be awkward when, not infrequently, the person calling the cab company for her must hold on the line for 5 minutes before the dispatcher takes the call. At work, she can read print well enough to compensate for much of what she misses auditorily; she can use a telephone with an amplifier or her TTY or MCM (telecommunication devices) for much of her outside telephoning. When such equipment is not suitable or effective, a secretary to whom Joan has taught sign language can help partially by interpreting the calls.

She does have difficulty lipreading her boss, a heavily accented native of Germany with a bushy mustache. She also misses out on office chatter, but since she works with people sensitive to those with disabilities (several others in the office are in wheelchairs or on crutches), she finds them generally patient and willing to fill her in on what she does not hear. She sometimes uses an interpreter in meetings and lectures, but her understanding of signs is still not adequate to be a total solution. Often she manages by using her "spyglass," a powerful monocular device; with it, she can do some lipreading. At board meetings for the arts and wilderness project, she has circumvented the problem to a degree by accepting the position of secretary. Someone else takes notes at the meetings while she tries to piece together what is happening by listening, lipreading with her spyglass, and watching the man write the notes. Later, as she types the notes into the minutes, she fills herself in on what she has missed.

In general, Joan can communicate very well in one-to-one situations. In groups, however, she is left out. She has often found herself enjoying a conversation with a companion until a third person approaches; then they seem to forget her. She says it makes her feel like shouting, "Talk to me!" but she continues, "You can't fill yourself up with that all the time or you do even less communicating. You can't keep making a pest out of yourself. So on some people, you just give up."

Even with her parents, who are otherwise extremely supportive of her and with whom she enjoys a good relationship, communication becomes a frustration. She has tried to get them to learn sign language so that she would have people to practice with; she has urged them, both verbally and with illustrated cards taped to the refrigerator, to learn fingerspelling so that conversations would not arrive at Joan's asking, about the crucial, missed word, "What?" and their repeating it, her asking again, "What?" and their repeating it louder and more carefully; her asking again.... In what probably describes many family relationships for hearing impaired individuals, she says, "They're not refusing to learn fingerspelling, they just don't do it. They understand how serious the problem is, but they don't understand how serious the problem is, if you know what I mean." When she misses a large part of the dinner table conversation, Joan and her mother will sit down together later and "rehash" what was said. Joan seems to reconcile herself to the situation partly with the feeling that much of what she misses is either repetitive or not particularly interesting.

As far as talking about more deep-seated concerns, she says that she and her mother have an unspoken agreement not to venture into topics connected with the disabilities. She does share some of her feelings with a neighbor who has a retarded son and a friend who volunteers with the social-recreational group, and those women also confide in her. But she says basically that she has never been comfortable talking about her problems, and in fact, she is more often in the role of listener and helper for her friends.

The questions of how to cope with a disability, of what constitutes acceptance or denial of one's status and limitations, are complex. Rehabilitation personnel who know Joan feel—not as critics, but objectively, as observers—that she does not fully accept her disabilities. She does not carry a blind person's cane. Instead, she follows the cues of other pedestrians or relies on her vision after using her spyglass to determine the color of traffic lights. She prefers to walk several blocks out of her way to cross at regulated intersections. She admits that, because she cannot perceive depth, when there are no traffic lights within a reasonable distance, she sometimes spends several minutes waiting for cars parked half a block away to pass. The disadvantage of her spyglass is that in magnifying what is straight ahead, it blocks what she would normally be able to see with peripheral vision; she cannot see traffic to either side. Some rehabilitation workers who have seen Joan walking on the street are amazed that she has not been seriously injured by an automobile.

Joan does not want to use a blind person's cane. She points out, with a note of triumph, that legally she cannot use one for she is not legally blind. She does not want other bus passengers to feel obligated to give her their seats. She has been the victim of one rape attempt since moving to Seattle, after which she says that *even* the social worker who has tried to convince her to use a white cane "admitted that in some situations a cane can be a detriment. Some people prey on those who look helpless." Joan acknowledges that in the wintertime, when she leaves work in the dark, she needs an aid. She plans, however, to use her large aluminum walking stick from her leg injury. She compares carrying a blind person's cane to having an umbrella–if you need it, you use it; if you don't, it gets left on the bus. Of course, being hit by a car and getting wet are consequences of dubious equivalence.

Her firmness about her capabilities without the cane seems comparable to her contention that she gets sufficient information when she is in a group meeting. She maintains that much of the discussion is repetitive or unimportant and, by combining what she can lipread with her spyglass and what she can hear, she understands all of the important contributions. She says that she will develop her sign language to the point of fluency when she needs it. For many situations, she seems to need it now. Sitting in a meeting with her, one feels with excruciating certainty that Joan cannot be receiving all that she says or believes she does. To catch her attention, people shout her name at volumes much louder than what they have been using throughout the meeting, and she does not respond. Although she uses the spyglass, much of the time people are not positioned so that she can see their mouths.

It seems, also, that Joan's reluctance to discuss any emotional effects of her disabilities–to describe the times when she was dejected or to postulate any influence they have had on her development—is related to a lack of acceptance. She closes discussion of the topic of emotional reactions with an acknowledgment that, yes, in the past she has been depressed, and "That's one reason why I'm not letting myself get into that bind again." She goes on, "You can foul yourself up—you can worry so much, that you can't do things that you ordinarily would be able to do simply because you're so upset about something you can't change."

If Joan does not completely accept her limitations, she seems nonetheless to be adjusted to them. If her denial, or rejection, causes her a certain amount of added frustration, it may also provide the impetus to remain as self-sufficient and normal as she can. Other people who, like Joan, have a disability with an uncertain course seem to develop attitudes similar to hers. They exasperate the family and friends who are certain they would be better of in a wheelchair—better off physically. But the individual's contention, by his behavior if not in words, is that psychologically he is better off fighting the disabilities, even if the fight requires denying the extent of the limitations.

Sometimes Joan's reasonably-stated explanations of what she does and why seem like evasions or rationalizations; yet they also contain an element that makes sense. We discussed the pattern that mental health workers delineate as the standard and necessary adjustment to changes in life—the loss of a loved person, the introduction of a physical disability. Those stages are disbelief and denial followed by anger, bargaining, mourning, and finally, acceptance. Joan says, "I don't fit the pattern of adjustment, maybe partly because I've never reached a final stage of the hearing or vision loss."

"I was almost completely blind as a child and I got my sight back. The hearing has always changed so gradually, you're not aware of it. I used to get colds and they would do the same thing to me (she would lose more hearing), but then it would come back up. I never knew if it were just a cold or if it were permanent. There have been periods when it was fluctuating and what I heard this week, I couldn't hear next week. The times I'm thinking of, maybe you're adjusting internally, but the external—the actual problem—is changing. The hearing comes up again.

"With my type of hearing loss, you're never sure where you're going. You just stop thinking about change and hold on—you get numb, you live from day to day. You know that whatever is happening isn't complete yet. It's more of a wait-and-see attitude. You just concentrate on what you can do. I don't rely on things more than I have to. You maintain your abilities better if you don't use any more aids than you absolutely have to. I'm going to use all of my sight while I have it.

"I get tired of people who focus on the emotional problems. Basically, a handicapped person is just a normal person with a few extra problems to cope with. This is my approach. Do I do something because of the handicap? Possibly; probably not; I don't know. I probably would have studied something quite different. But my personality, I don't know. It's hard to answer because presumptions are shaped by what you are. If you are handicapped, that's part of it. There aren't things I really regret. Maybe not getting married and having kids. But I don't know if that's because of the handicap. I can't say if there's a cause and effect. It's like asking someone from the city what he'd be like if he were from the country."

Joan uses the word "cope" differently from most people. Whereas others usually use it to mean how they have dealt emotionally with problems in their lives, she uses the word to refer to her practical solutions to problems—she has coped by getting better hearing aids, she will cope by improving her sign language. Joan's approach is to be practical and pertinacious. Watching her travel or in a meeting, coaxing her to discuss emotional reactions, one becomes frustrated because she seems to ignore reality. Yet ultimately one must acknowledge that she has found an effective way of dealing with her situation and respect her for it. She sums up her philosophy, "I think the best plan is to do the best you can and stop stewing."

Ross Adams

"My problem is congenital. It's my understanding it didn't show up until I was 12 years old and it got more pronounced when I was a teenager. My fixation point of vision got down to five degrees and now, to the present day, it's remained that way. When I graduated from deaf school in 1950, I was 19 and it has remained five degrees ever since then–both eyes. I've been hard of hearing all my life.

"Before I became a Christian, I was thinking about the now, now and have pleasure, good times and comfortable feelings. I was kind of unstable and complaining a lot. But we are here for a purpose, you know, and sometimes God will give you strength through weakness. When I read all the Apostles, you know, they had a lot of trouble themselves, but they kept on to overcome it. Adversity, you know, it may be more of a blessing. It's better hope when you have a struggle in life. Life is not a bed of roses, you know. You've got to expect the road to be a little bumpy. If it's first too smooth you might get complacent and you might go astray and do wrong. If you want to go the narrow way, sometimes you have to have a lot of adversity before you, so you can succeed."

Ross Adams is a 47-year-old bachelor. He lives in Fort Worth, Texas with his mother. In contrast to her tiny, delicate appearance, he is a very tall, slightly overweight man. His hair is greying and his complexion is pale, but he looks healthy. His placid face resembles that of a younger man and sometimes, because of a kind of boyish charm, he seems much younger than he is. At other times, though—ironically, when Mrs. Adams "mothers" him, straightening his tie or admonishing him to wear a raincoat—he seems less like a son and more like half of an older couple, comfortable in their shared habits, relishing their friendly disagreements.

Ross has a Texan drawl and an amiable southern politeness. When he misses a remark, he gently queries, "Ma'am?" Despite the firmness with which he offers his opinions, he is mild mannered. He likes to jest, but the quips come too fast when he is ill at ease. His speech is interspersed with "you know," and its frequency, too, is a good clue to which topics make him nervous. He is open, though, and, one senses, painstakingly honest with himself.

One person who knows Ross describes him as neither deaf nor hearing, blind nor sighted. His hearing loss is great enough to have required education at the Texas School for the Deaf. With the hearing aids he now wears, he can use the telephone; listen to the radio, record player, and television; and understand loud speech. *Retinitis pigmentosa* caused night blindness and limited his peripheral vision early in his life, but it left clear central sight, a "pinpoint" as Ross describes it. In recent years, cataracts have clouded that over, although during the past two summers he has had operations to remove them that have successfully restored the vision on which he depends. For Ross to comprehend a conversation, one must either sit closely and speak loudly, almost shouting at him, or at a distance of 10 to 15 feet and sign. When he left the state school for the deaf, he barely used his voice. Since he has been in the business world, however, he has developed his speech to the point that now it is clear and understandable. Although he is apprehensive about mispronouncing words, he rarely does so.

Ross became a Christian 18 years ago. "I was baptized in the Church of Christ about 1960. Some people came up from Austin to establish a church for the deaf here. Really, when I met them, I was just going to the Methodist Church as a ritual, not learning God's word at all, not studying, not reading the Bible. So they showed me a few things, you know, like Baptism. You're supposed to be immersed in water, you know, for remission of sins. I got to studying and found out a lot of Methodist teaching is not right, not following God's pattern of living. So I left the Methodist Church and started going to this Church of Christ. I found out you're supposed to worship in spirit and truth, you know; that's the only way to please God. I started reading the Bible and I found comfort. We have to make the most of what we have. I decided to live with my handicap because there's nothing I can do about it. It's congenital; you're born with it. I found I've been blessed with good health generally; I haven't been sick very much in my whole life. And I found that all people have to suffer at one time or another. I read where Paul said he wanted thorns, you know, in the flesh, that he would learn strength through weakness. It would teach him humility so he wouldn't be so haughty-minded. Sometimes when people are well and think nothing's wrong with them, they get so puffed up and boisterous because of their good fortune. They might not be humble of other people."

Ross' Christianity is a core of beliefs reflecting his attitudes not only toward struggle and acceptance of difficulty, but also toward propriety and family relationships. When he was a year old, his mother, discovering that his father had been unfaithful, told Mr. Adams to leave. Ross says that his older brother, Ogden, then 6, was old enough to feel somewhat bitter toward their father. Ross did not understand the situation at the time, but as he grew older, he had a poignant sense of missing a certain family unity. "It's a strange thing to have divided loyalty and love. You feel like you're a go-between sometimes; one or the other is trying to wring a confession from you. Each one of them was craving for their children's affection more than the other. It felt a little lonely you know. I kind of stifled myself–not express my feeling too much, don't talk about it–just try to go home like nothing happened. But I noticed these things and kind of felt awkward. So you're always conscious of what you say and careful not to offend one or the other. You want to love both of 'em, you know, so you don't express yourself truly. You kind of suppress you feelings."

His mother was aware of his hearing loss from the time that Ross was a toddler, but she felt that he could succeed in a regular public school classroom. When he reached the first grade, however, his teacher advised her to send him to the school for the deaf, for he was thirsty to learn and missing too much in class. He experienced academic problems at the school for the deaf, too. Some of his teachers signed, but with others he had to depend on lipreading and residual hearing. He did not wear a hearing aid when he was in school and thus could not hear as well as he does now; with the vision impairment, he could not always see clearly. Ross believes that educators and people in general do not understand the complexity of a partial sensory loss; although his teachers realized that the deaf students would miss information, they expected Ross to learn without any trouble.

His eyesight presented social difficulties as well. "Before I was 12 years old, I had a pretty wide scope. I can remember that I could see anything around. When I got 12, things started to change. But I was just a child and I thought that was a normal process, part of growing up. I thought things change. People take for granted their eyes. They can do anything they want; they don't think anything can happen. I had hard trouble in school. A lot of them didn't understand. Sometimes they're waving at me and they think I'm ignoring them or acting ugly. I knew something was wrong when my eyes got real bad, and I couldn't compete in normal activities, socializing with others. I just had very few friends. They can be nice to you, but they're not actually friends."

Ross' response to his discomfort was not unlike his reaction to the pressure he had felt as a result of his parents' separation. "When you can't see at night, you know, when you've got r.p. trouble, you kind of feel you can't go out and have a good night life. Since you don't have night vision, you know, you don't see nothing. The kids don't understand night blindness because none of 'em had it, except one boy and he was more like me. He stayed to himself and declined friendships, going places after dark. You don't gain a lot of friendships when you decline invitations like that. I got to a point where they started talking that Ross wanted to be alone, so leave him alone. I tried, but I felt more comfortable to be alone in a lot of situations."

Ross says that he was somewhat wild in school, defiant and frequently breaking regulations. Two or three times he sneaked out at night, despite his blindness, to the minor league baseball games, earning demerits that he had to work off on weekends. Looking back, he believes that his misbehavior was not simply frivolous–because he was different, but not noticeably so, perhaps he was trying to attract the attention and concern of school personnel. He says, also, that when you are withdrawn but want more friends, you respond quickly and perhaps unwisely to those who show an interest.

Though he tended to avoid most activities, Ross was determined to stay involved in the sport that he truly loved. "I still managed to play baseball. I started to play when I was 13 and I played every position except first base. I wound up as a pitcher and I think I played better in that position than any others. In baseball, you're not around anybody. You're on your own, individual. You only have to watch for the ball. Even with a pinpoint of vision, you can still follow the flight of the ball." During his last year of high school, he was chosen to try out for the Brooklyn Dodgers at their local camp. He was 1 of 5 finalists out of 100 boys. The scouts told him he had a good right arm, but they also noticed that he had poor balance and limited peripheral vision, and they turned him down. "My ambition was to succeed in baseball. I had a lot of talent and I wanted to be a ballplayer. I felt like, you know, if I didn't have this trouble, well, I might have made it somewhere. Probably not at the top. I probably would have made it in the minor leagues."

Ross was not interested in college or further "book learning" when he graduated from school. Though he was disappointed in missing out on a career in baseball, he feels that one scout's continued interest in him kept him from becoming discouraged and giving up. He looked for other work and, with training in printing from his school, he found a job in that field. He worked briefly for one firm, but could not "navigate too well" and they let him go. He then worked as a mail clerk for 2 weeks, but when his employer required him to drive, his poor vision again led to dismissal. Feeling more and more disheartened, he nonetheless applied for a job at the First National Bank of Fort Worth. At first, the officer who interviewed him said they had no openings, but as Ross was leaving, he called him back and said, "We might have an opening in bookkeeping in 2 weeks. Come on June 1st." Ross did, and he has been at the bank, in that department, for the past 27 years.

He began as a bookkeeper, became a poster (typing information on monthly statements), and is now the Internal Records Control Clerk. He microfilms all documents that go through the bank; he also picks up reports from Data Processing and passes them out to the appropriate staff members.

A taxicab, paid for by the bank, comes to his home each morning at 5:30 a.m. and drives him to the bank 10 minutes away. Ross requested to work those early hours because he is more efficient working alone. He is also less self-conscious than later in the day. "I feel apprehension when I have to walk around with people there. A lot of people are passing by and I kind of have to look all around. Like when anybody's walking with me to the coffee place. I usually look at a person when they're talking, you know, to see what they're talking about, but I can't do that when I'm walking because I'll run into somebody. The coffee shop and cafeteria are dim-lighted. When I walk through different shades of light, it's a little confusing to me. When you have retina damage, you can't change the focus. You don't see as you should be seeing for a period of time. So I just try to decline an invitation to go and just stay put at my work station and, you know, try to avoid a situation like that, you know, that might make it embarrassing for myself and others."

"I guess I have a complex of inferiority. There's a lot of things going on, conversations at the bank and I don't hear all of 'em. When you're hard of hearing, you know, it's natural to have a little suspicion when you can't hear what they're talking about. But maybe I'm better off because sometimes they tell dirty jokes, you know, and I don't go along with it. Before I became a Christian, I kind of permitted it, condoned it, because I laughed along with it. But in time, when you tolerate that thing going on, you know, they think you're part of the group, and that's unbecoming a Christian when you allow those things to go on."

Ross has accumulated more than 1 full year of sick leave at the bank. Until his first operation for cataracts, he had taken only 9 days of sick leave in 25 years of work. He used half of them when he was hit by a bus while walking home from work and he had to see a chiropractor for traction treatments. Last summer he was out 9 more days for his operation and convalescence. This year he planned to use his 2 week's vacation for his second hospital stay and recovery. To his disappointment, he had to stay out of work longer until his eye muscles learned to work together again, and he had to use sick leave, too. Ross jokes about his reluctance to miss work–that the bank may be so impressed with his temporary replacement's performance that he might find himself out of a job–but he also has serious concerns. "Well, you know, I feel like a handicapped person should be . . . try to be good. I feel dependability goes a long way. If I'm out, you know, they'll think I'm losing a loyalty or something. If I'm weak in some areas, my dependability will probably support me to continue my position there. I notice a lot of these hearing, they get along, nothing wrong with them, they can take off, you know; but they expect a lot more from a handicapped person. They expect them to do about twice as good maybe. I've always had that feeling . . . we have to do more maybe."

When asked if he is happy with his job, Ross answers, "Well, I know my limitations. When you don't see well enough . . . I've learned you'd better accept your lot. I feel I could probably do better. I think about being an accountant. My math wasn't very good in school, but I might do better now, buckle down and study, you know. I've got a cousin from Tennessee who's an accountant so I took an interest in learning, thought maybe I'd probably make a better living by becoming one, you know, and draw a little bit more of a salary. Now I kind of have to move about a lot and feel like it's a little pressured job; you have to get it out real quick and I can't do it in 1 hour, you know. I just can't see everything. They told me at the Goodrich Center for the Deaf that the Blind Commission will help me take a course in accounting or anything I want. If I feel like I want to better myself vocationally I might look into it. But I've thought over again. Sometimes the more money you get, you get more greedy and you might have a bad appetite in the wrong way, so I don't know."

"I feel like it's pretty monotonous doing the same thing all the time but I've stuck with it and paid this home and left a lot of money in the bank, saved, you know. When you can't drive, you can't go places, you have to think about the location and, you know, the bank's been good to me. They're paying my transportation. If you've got five degrees of vision, you can't drive, and you want to be a ballplayer, but you can't play . . . you don't have enough vision to play, so you've got to accept what you can do in a limited area. That cuts down on a lot of possibilities of what you can do. But when I see ten million people out of work I'm not bad off, you know. And not very many people who have my vision are able to hold down jobs. I have learned to accept difficulty and go along. Another reason is the bank's been good to me . . . and if they think this is the best I can do, I'll just try to be content and make the most of it. So I have a mixture of feelings about that. Maybe it's better to hold on to what you've got. Sometimes if you want to get ahead, you've got to take a long shot in the deep; 'cause life is a gamble, you've got to put an effort behind it. But I think I'm a little lazy. I don't long shot, but try to be content with what I've got."

One reason Ross would like to earn more money is to be better able to support a wife and family. He maintains a staunch commitment to the importance of the institutions of marriage and family, but he is doubtful about marrying and raising children himself. "I'd like to have happiness in life, you know. It's not good for a man to live alone. God did not intend for a man to be alone. I believe that no man can be totally content unless he has what he wants, a helpmate in life and all that, you know. When you have problems, it's better to share with somebody who might listen. Then you have two heads to solve the problem. But you know, I've been advised, my condition is genetic, you know, and if you have children, they may have the same condition thing. You don't want them to go through life suffering like you did and so, if I don't get married I can't have children. So I just kind of refrain from proposing to any girl, you know. There are a lot of girls I like, and there's one particular I like. She doesn't know it, but when I never could marry her, I could not try to string her along too far."

"Apostle Paul was a bachelor, you know, and God said, 'Paul, it's better to marry than to burn.' You know, if you can control and contain yourself, then you don't need to be married. He's not saying you are required to be married. If you can control your life and not fall into fornication, you know, then it's all right not to be married. So since I'm able to contain myself, why I don't have to worry about it.

"You know about that liberation movement that's going

on. They frown on an institution like marriage. They carry on like they can have sex outside the family and marriage. You know, that's just a violation of God's laws. That should be combined in marriage and a home. And they have an unnatural affection, going around with somebody of the same sex. You know a woman is made for a man. You know, that's written. They should be a helpmate. People can express their own opinions, but when they try to conflict with God's laws ... God has the last authority to say what's best for the home and for the family.

"I'm not that lonely, you know, but I'm lonely in the sense that I don't have companionship. When my mother be gone one of these days and I'll be all alone here, I can't cook, you know. You need somebody to see about that. Mother's not well, you know, and one of these days, you know.... So I will probably have to do something drastic when she's gone. I'll have to have a helpmate. But I don't know if anybody'll put up with me with my condition. If she wants to have healthy children, and most of 'em want children.... It's not good not to have a child when you're married. But now, well, mother's all alone, you know. I recognize that she's been good to me all these years and I feel like I should repay, you know, return all the goodness she showed me. She practically raised us boys alone. If you don't provide for your family, you're worse than an infidel. That's in the Bible, you know. And it's just not good to have your in-laws live in the same house. So I don't see much chance of marrying while she's still living. But see, I'm still young. A man's never old 'til he reaches mid-fifty, maybe, and it's still not too late for me, is it?"

Ross is satisfied with his social life now. He leaves the bank at 2:00 or 2:30 p.m., depending upon the volume of work. After work, he is content to stay at home listening to records, watching TV, or talking with friends on the phone. He keeps up with the news through the daily paper and enjoys reading religious literature.

Ogden, his older brother, comes down from Tennessee with his wife and children for a week each summer. He has made special trips the past 2 years to visit Ross in the hospital. Ross regrets that Ogden has not followed his example by joining the Church of Christ as his mother and some other relatives in Tennessee have done. He also admits that he sometimes feels inferior to his brother, who is vice-president of an insurance company, is well-educated, and can talk about "anything under the sun." Mostly, though, Ross just feels proud to have a brother who has always treated him with love and respect.

Ross sometimes goes to the Center for the Deaf for their afternoon social hour, but he must stand at some distance from other people to read their signs. He becomes embarrassed when, because of his limited close up vision, he cannot piece together the patches of faces that he sees to recognize people he should know. He used to have many deaf people coming to his house for religious advice, but when they began to come as a group, both Ross and his mother were uncomfortable, and he discouraged them from continuing their visits so often.

Ross is a "free-lance chess player" in Fort Worth, with the opportunity to play quite frequently. He recently beat a local champion in four straight games. In addition, he usually plays several times a month with a friend who he has known since he was a boy, another hard of hearing man with vision problems. The other man likes to talk about women, "what makes them tick," and Ross enjoys that and their discussions about books. They used to play together more often than they do now, but as Ross has begun to beat him consistently, his friend has lost some enthusiasm. Ross plans to build up his friend's confidence to compete again. He worries a bit about the other man, for although he is very smart, he is not working now and cannot find a job. Ross just keeps trying to encourage him, as he does an epileptic friend at the bank.

As for himself, he says, "Sometimes I feel like, if I had good vision, I could be gregarious, you know, have personality, but when you can't do these things, you try to subdue your openness a little bit. You try to live a restricted life. When I look back, I think most people have tried to be nice. Sometimes they don't understand, but I don't fault them. If you don't tell them, they won't know. When I was younger, I didn't understand the problem myself. But now I kind of understand the problem and the relationship with other people. I don't force myself on anyone. I just be calm and know I'm still working... and they seem to like me there at the bank, so I'm really content. Maybe it's better to enter life maimed than be in perfect body, because that body, when it dies, will be put in a lake of fire. So learn to live with it and then, after this life is finished, we put on a new body, a more perfect body, and all our ills and problems will be taken away. It doesn't mean when you become a Christian that you'll be without problems. You'll have problems, but you'll have better understanding to cope."

Mike Price

Mike Price is in his early twenties. He is tall, broad shouldered, and very handsome. He lives in a suburb of a large city and walks to his job as an assembler for an electronics firm. Although Mike is diagnosed as having Usher's Syndrome, his hearing loss is not so profound as to prevent him from hearing and understanding speech, provided he is in a quiet environment, using his hearing aids, and those with him are talking somewhat louder than what is usual in conversation. Mike speaks, but he has to remind himself not to mumble, and he has some difficulty pronouncing the words that he does not hear clearly.

His vision is impaired by the night blindness and tunnel vision of *retinitis pigmentosa*, and by inoperable cataracts in both eyes. Within the past year, he has become totally blind in his right eye, and he has a field restriction and only blurry perception in the left. In a good lighting situation, with careful positioning of the person communicating with him, Mike can combine what he hears, lipreads, and, for those who use sign language, what he reads on their hands, to be included in the conversation. At other times though, when he is in a dimly-lit restaurant where there is a background hum of noise, for example, he is virtually totally deaf and blind, and can receive communication only through the tactile method of signing that he is beginning to practice.

Mike is not willing to have information about his current life published, for some of his relationships, particularly those with older women, are complex, and he feels that outsiders are not likely to understand him. He agreed, however, to share his experiences from the time he was in school—both the 10 or 12 years he spent at a state residential school for the deaf and his 2 years of college at Gallaudet. His account of the treatment he received from other people and its influence on his development may, of course, be biased by his own perceptions and memory. At the same time, many of the very positive attitudes he now expresses appear to be solutions that he recognizes intellectually, but does not always incorporate into his behavior. Nonetheless, his story seems important, for Mike explains in detail what most other people with Usher's Syndrome often allude to—teasing and rejection from other students, lack of understanding from school personnel, and an early preference to be alone.

"I had lots of problems in school and with my family. First, when I started, I went to a hearing school for the first and second grades. I don't remember the name of the school and stuff like that, but I know I didn't do well at all. The teacher knew that I wasn't able to learn or keep up with things in the classroom, and I didn't get along with the other kids; we couldn't communicate. So I left that school, but my parents didn't know what to do. They didn't think of sending me to a deaf school because they didn't know anything about it. (Mike's family lived on a farm at that time; one of his three older sisters also has a hearing impairment, but she was able to continue in public schools.) Well, I wasted some of my time then because I just stayed home and worked on the farm when I was about 7 or 8 years old. I don't remember when I started at the school for the deaf and blind. I was at least 8 or 9 years old, no less than that." Mike's school, like several others in the country, was established for both blind and deaf students; their classrooms, dormitories, and activities, however, are separated, and the two groups rarely have any contact.

"I guess from the beginning I was having vision problems. The most I knew, I couldn't see in the dark. I was always getting behind other people when we were going places. I got behind, and I was the last person to come along until I could find my way. I began to be really frustrated with that, and I thought I was the only one in the world. I didn't know anybody else who had similar problems, except for the blind people in the other department, and we weren't living together. But sometimes I'd look at them and wonder if I'm like them or not.

"I noticed that I bumped into people from sideways. Sometimes I thought they were bumping into me and didn't realize that I was the one that just didn't see them. Or they'd wave at me and say I'm always stuck up. I just couldn't get over that. When they started calling me names like that, I began to move my head and look around to catch what was happening, and they'd call me more names and say, 'You're suspicious, suspicious.' It wasn't true. I was just trying to help myself.

"I used to play ball, and at first I thought I was better than a lot of my friends, but I began to realize when they started talking about me, or the coach started complaining, I began to realize that I made a lot of mistakes. I'd bump into people. I didn't see everything at one time, or I'd miss a few things, like a ball passed me and I didn't know it was coming my way. Whenever I could see the ball at the right time or in the right place, I did well. When I couldn't, I did kind of sloppy or bad to other people.

"I got frustrated, and when I was a little older, I was beginning to have a hard time with the other kids, because I guess we didn't accept each other. I didn't understand them and they didn't understand me. I'd complain to people a lot, but they didn't understand; or they didn't want to listen; or they didn't think it was important. And I didn't know what to tell them. I couldn't see, but I didn't know what I couldn't see, and with r.p., your eyes don't look blind. I think there were a lot of misunderstandings–them and me.

"The more problems I had, the harder it was to solve them. I didn't have many friends. When I got into junior high and high school, it got to where I didn't want to go to the parties or go places in the dark. I just didn't do a lot of things that most kids do because I remembered the things when I was growing up, and everything I'd do, I'd get frustrated or down or depressed. I didn't think it was worth it to try to do things because I just didn't know how to deal with them or how to enjoy them, unless I was with some friends who knew me, and I could be comfortable. That would be maybe the only time I'd do things. I just usually stayed in my room all the time.

"When I was in my freshman year of high school, I think I was beginning to be more mature, but by then it didn't seem to help because it was harder for other people to understand me. You know, I'm talking about gym and football... anytime I'd do something wrong, or bump into people, they'd think about that and remind themselves about things that happened before. People made fun of me. Instead of my name sign with an *M* on my shoulder for Mike, they made it with the sign for *blind*, and they tapped everybody on the shoulder with *blind, blind*. Kids can be cruel. I called them my friends, but they could have been my worst enemies.

"Or else people would overlook me, just not pay attention to me. It may have been normal for them because they really didn't understand me at all. Nobody really understood what the problem was. I didn't either. I just felt I was left in the hole and nothing could be right. I had to rough it out, and I didn't know how. Maybe because I wasn't smart enough, or I just didn't have the information that could tell me what was wrong.

"One time in a basketball game it was the most embarrassing time, I think, in my whole life, especially because of the coaches. We had a tournament. We were in the second position, and it was the last game. We couldn't finish it because there was a bad storm and a blackout. I had only one friend, and I knew where he was before the lights went out. He wasn't too far, so I ran to look for him to hold his elbow, and I told him what was wrong. I couldn't see in the dark. So he helped me and we went to this waiting room. When the lights went back on, everybody started laughing at me, even the coaches—I had two of them, and they just laughed. 'Oh, did you see Mike... he was looking, looking, he couldn't find his way, he finally grabbed hold of Don.' I was just standing there. I couldn't even stand up for myself. Everybody was just laughing. I really hurt a lot. It was hell for me, suffering like that. And things just didn't seem to get better.

"I went to counselors, but the people I talked to didn't ask me questions like, 'What's wrong with your vision?' All they asked was why I had so many emotional problems. I tried to tell them why but.... I kept trying to tell the teachers in my own words, in my own vocabulary, what was wrong, *why* I had so many problems, but nobody could understand. There were some teachers there that I really liked, I really admired, and I think that there was one teacher who believed that I just couldn't see well and she did what she could. But all the other teachers in the school thought I just had a bad attitude. I don't think I had a bad attitude; I just didn't know how to tell people what was the matter.

"A lot of times in class, people would tease me and the teacher would say, 'Why don't you get up close to the board?' But that wouldn't help. I just was never comfortable. My teachers said, 'Wear glasses.' It didn't matter if I wore glasses. I told them the doctor said this is all they could do for me; the glasses I had were as strong as they could make. It didn't matter how thick the glasses were. If they were any thicker, I wouldn't have seen at all; it would have been all blurred. I had people tease me because my glasses were way out like that.

"I don't know how I learned in class. I got through, but what they did with me, they just kind of kept me. They didn't really put me where I should have belonged, and I wasn't getting anywhere. They let me miss a lot of things and just go on. There were times when I couldn't-like math-I could do some of the harder math, but I couldn't do some of the basics. I really couldn't see the board at all. Using what I heard was the best learning method for me. And of course reading, what I could read.

"Most of the teachers talked and signed, so I could hear some of them. But there were several deaf teachers who just signed and the students just signed. I had a hell of a time. I didn't get good grades. They always put me in the lowest class, but I was just as smart as anybody else ... if I'd had a chance to learn. Maybe part of it was I didn't want to, but I don't think so. I think that I was so frustrated that I became less enthusiastic. And so you just sit there in class and daydream. I know I'm not dumb. Whatever I learned, I could understand well. But that was about the only information I could collect unless I wanted to go home and study. Really, if I couldn't hear, I would have missed everything. I think people would have thought I was retarded or crazy and sent me to the mental hospital.

"I took a driving course in my junior year. I *knew* right there that I didn't want to drive because the teacher said I was always going off the lane. I couldn't park right. In front of the building where he wanted me to park, I would always come too close and hit the building, and he'd get mad. I think they thought I had a bad attitude or I was angry with them. It wasn't that; I'd just get so frustrated. I didn't know how to deal with it. The teacher even grabbed hold of my shirt, and then I really got angry, 'cause that scared me. I didn't know how to tell them that I just couldn't do it. They asked me, 'Why? why? why?' and they'd always think that I was 'a quitter, a quitter.' But I just thought it's better if you quit, 'cause if I stuck in there, everybody would get me angry and I'd start fighting.

"I think my junior year was my most unhappy year. Some girls who I wanted to be with never wanted to be with me, and I don't know, I just got really frustrated and unhappy. I was anxious to finish school. I was just tired of being there.

"When I finished high school, I was accepted at Gallaudet. People talked me into going. They said, 'No matter what the problem is, go anyway.' Not only that, I didn't have anything else to do, and I couldn't get along with my dad. When I was in school, I used to go home on the weekend. I would rather be home than at school. At school, I didn't have anything I could do. Home I could take walks or go bike riding unless the weather was bad and I couldn't go out.

"But my family is the kind that never smiles. My father was always angry and complained about everything. He just always did things the hard way. I think that's where I got some of my attitudes, too, being negative. My family is like that. But I'm trying to change now. My dad was really rough on me. He would shove me, push me around. He would never sit down and talk with me, never. Things got pretty bad. My deaf sister and I would talk about the problems around the house and why. She and I signed; we were the only ones who could really communicate. Everybody in my family is much older than me. My father's old enough to be my grandfather, and my sisters were all dating and getting married when I was young, so I really never knew them. I was closest to my mother.

"I went to Gallaudet in 1974, but I don't think I was really prepared to go, because even though I passed my courses, I had some weaknesses, and I knew I would have a hard time there because I didn't have a good high school education. And I think I was scared, too, because I didn't know what to do. I still didn't understand what was wrong with me. I just thought I was the only one in the world. And I hated to go because of other kids I knew in high school who were there. I didn't want to see my old classmates because of the way they treated me in high school. Even when I got to Gallaudet, they wouldn't speak to me, and they'd tell other people, 'Oh, that guy isn't important, don't pay any attention to him.'

"And it was more trouble because my family didn't support me. I told them I couldn't see, but the only one who ever really took it seriously was my mother. That's just the character of my family. We don't believe things, or don't accept what other people say. They didn't want me to go to college anyway. If I ever complete it, I'll be the first child, and there's only two in our relatives who did.

"My first year at Gallaudet was hard. I had some friends, mostly multiply-handicapped students—one guy in a wheelchair I played chess with. There were some girls I was friends with, and I could go to their rooms and talk. But I had a lot of problems, and I was really angry and emotional and got into fights.

"The summer in between my two years of college, I had trouble with my family. Things had just built up on me for so many years. I knew every time that I wanted to know what happened or wanted to ask, 'What happened over there?' other people wouldn't tell me. They could see and hear and knew exactly what happened, and I would just be standing there and have no idea.

"What happened that summer, we were playing horseshoes—me, my dad, my brother-in-law, and one of the neighbors, Gary. Gary's son was outside playing. He knocked down another boy. Well, the boy's father came out of his house and knocked down Gary's son, because Gary's son knocked his son down. Gary ran over. I didn't know; I was just playing horseshoes. I didn't see him leave, and I didn't know he was gone 'til I looked up and saw he was missing.

"Pretty soon, I saw my dad looking over that way, and my brother-in-law looking over that way, and I looked that way, but there were cars down the street and it was hard for me to see the depth or tell what was happening. I didn't know there were kids out there 'til later.

"So I was getting really anxious to know what was happening, but I thought, well, if I ask, they won't tell me; that's the way they are. They just don't understand. I think sometimes they think that I'm dumb and it's just not worth it. I'm not dumb. If I were dumb, I wouldn't be curious and asking what's happening. I feel like I need to know what's happening to satisfy myself.

"My dad and brother-in-law were together and talking. I think sometimes I'm jealous because my brother-in-law and my dad can communicate and they do a lot of things together. More than they do with me. I think that hurt me some ways. But they were talking and talking, and I'm sure they were talking about what was happening and they knew what it was. So I came up to my brother-in-law and said, 'What's happening over there?' And he said, 'Oh, nothing.'

"I got very pissed off. I said, 'You're my brother-in-law and you just treat me like a slave or something.' I was mad. I didn't get an answer to what was happening, and here they understood it. They left me out. I picked up a rock and threw it down, just to get it out of my system. I wasn't throwing it at them. My brother-in-law didn't realize that. I threw it down and it bounced up. I think it hit him. I think that's what happened. But he gave me a shove. Right there, I just exploded. That's where the fight started. He was wrestling me, my dad was wrestling me. They were fighting me—but that wasn't solving the problem. I think they were trying to calm me down, but that wasn't going to do it. Gary came over and there were three against me.

"Boy, I was getting stronger and tougher, and I got hold of my dad's arm and I swung him. He was kind of flying in the air, real low above the cement on the driveway. He finally hit his head; his hat came off and he hit the ground. I was still angry, and I said, 'Keep your hands off me and leave me alone.' I told them when I'm angry like that, I don't want to be bothered, but they were still bothering me and yelling at me. I didn't see him, but Gary got behind me and was trying to pin my arms back. That made me a little more mad. It was hard for me, but I finally got him off. They gave up and didn't touch me anymore, but I wanted to show them that I *didn't want* them to touch me.

"We went into the house and I picked up a knife, a steak knife, and I had it in my hand. I was just trying to scare people. I wasn't going to attack them or anything. But my dad, he was gonna call the sheriff. I said, 'Just go ahead.'

Then my brother-in-law said, 'No, no, forget it.' So I finally left and walked about a mile to a girl that I knew. I went to see her and talked it over with her. After that, I had several more fights with my dad, and I even broke his glasses. He had cuts on his eyebrows. He tried to fight me back, but he couldn't.

"It was really an emotional experience. But I knew what I was doing. I wanted to get it out of my system and show people I was serious. But they thought I was crazy. They wanted to lock me up in the state hospital. I've just had a lot of emotional . . . especially when it's built up over so many years. I just didn't know any other way. I would have liked to have done it a nicer way, but I just didn't know how."

Mike went back to Gallaudet for a second year, and that is when he learned that he had Usher's Syndrome. "I started going to the infirmary. Back in high school I started that, just going sometimes and talking with the nurses. I did it again at Gallaudet, and finally I told one nurse about my high school life and how frustrated I was in the dark and things like that. She suspected that maybe I had r.p., because she knew Art Roehrig who worked at Gallaudet and had it. She thought maybe I had the same problem, so she volunteered to take me to the National Institutes of Health in Maryland. I spent 8 hours there with her as my interpreter. That's when I found out."

"I was really shocked. I couldn't believe it. I told the doctor, 'All this time and I didn't know. That was why I was so frustrated and unhappy.' After all those years. I don't know what it would have been like before if I'd known the problem better. I might have been the same, I don't know. But I was glad to find out. But it was also hard for me to believe the other stuff.

"First the doctor wanted to know if I wanted to see a counselor. He was a little bit worried; so was the nurse. But then he said okay, he would sit down and show me what was the matter. He had some demonstrating pictures and he showed me those and did some drawings of how much I could see, degrees, and stuff like that. I got the idea, but I just couldn't believe it—that was it. And he told me, maybe in 5 or 10 years from then I might become totally blind or something like that. He said, 'Your vision *will* get worse; there's no question about that.' He also told me about marriage and to be careful about what girl I marry. He said that I might give birth to a child with the same condition. And he explained about the dark and about my limitations. He told me a lot of things; I don't remember them all.

"Then it took me some time to realize how serious it was. I still have problems accepting it, but I think I had more problems at first because I didn't know *how* to accept it, until I learned there are a lot more people who have it. Now I can look at them and see how well they do. But it took me a long time. I think I was closeminded, and it took me a long time to become more openminded about it.

"I stayed at Gallaudet but I stopped going to classes. I guess I really didn't want to learn. I think I was pissed off. I didn't know what to do, whether to leave school or stay. Learning was really hard for me. I could understand if I wanted to, but I had to study hard to understand. I was having a lot of personal problems. I talked with my friends. One person would tell me to do one thing and another would tell me another thing. They wanted me to do this or that, and I didn't know who to follow. About my future—what should I do? What kind of teacher should I be? Should I work now? Or stay in school? They were mostly staff in the dormitory, some teachers and nurses. They all looked at me different and I didn't know who to follow or who could understand. It was like I was just left out in the ocean and didn't know what to do. I didn't want to go to counselors. I get tired of counselors. They do their job, but somehow, I'm just tired of it. I just rather be friends with people.

"I went back home and I was wishing I didn't. I had a lot of problems. Bad fights and arguments with my dad and brother-in-law. I wanted to be alone. I wanted to do what I wanted to do. They wanted me to go to work right off. They weren't able to help me or to understand. I just got there and boy, they were right on my back, pushing me. I was really depressed. Part of it was, before I came home, my mother was in the hospital for a week and they didn't let me know. They knew I was close to my mother and I would have wanted to come home. She had already died when I got there; the day I got there, she was already dead. That tore me up. I don't know what it was with my family. Communication or something. I think they didn't really like me. I think it's because of my attitudes. I really can't say how I acted, 'cause I can't see myself. I just know that's some of the reason."

Mike stayed with his father for a few months, trying to find a job through vocational rehabilitation. His rehabilitation counselor suggested that he go to the larger city that he lives near now to receive a full evaluation of his skills and needs for training. He moved, and has been living in that area for about 2 years. He has thought a lot about what would have helped him as a child and teenager to understand himself better. He feels that the two most crucial aids would have been accurate information about his limited vision and the support of his family.

Mike says, "I *wish* when I was growing up that somebody had come up to me and had a movie camera and didn't even let me know or see him taking pictures, for a whole day, everywhere, a lot of places with different people, then showed me the things that I missed and why I didn't see them. I think they should take movies of some of these students now and show the people who are normal–teachers and professionals–to help the students."

"He may have to have note takers and maybe the teachers are going to have to work a little bit harder. They need to find out if the student can see the boards, then change them or make extra copies of things for the student. The teachers get good pay; it's not gonna hurt for them to work a little bit more. I think they have to learn to be more patient. Then they can teach the student to take more responsibility for himself.

"But I think the family is the most important thing for the child. I think that my parents knew that I had r.p., but they never told me what the doctor said. I can't prove it, but I think so. The family has to work with the child when he's young. When he's depressed, they need to explain, 'Mike, I know you like basketball, but you know, when you're older, life's gonna be different for you. Now you may want to play basketball and be on the first string, but, you know, when you get older, it may not work out that way because of your limitation. But later you may want different things.'

"If I had a child with Usher's Syndrome, I would send him to a doctor more frequently than normal children to see if there's any change. That way you can kind of prepare for his future. I would do all kinds of things, play ball, play all kinds of sports that I could think of and see what he enjoys the most, and work with him, like a coach, even though when he's older, he may not be able to do a lot of those things. As he got older, I would explain it to him. I would always have my wife or me keep in touch with the teachers or the principal and find out how he's doing. If he's having problems, emotional problems, then we'd go to a counselor with him. I would go too, because there are some things I may not understand. I know all Usher's Syndrome is not the same. But if you work with kids when they're younger, then when they're older, they have a good chance to be a better person."

Mike still doesn't like to go to counselors, and he feels that they would be more useful to him if they came and watched his behavior in order to tell him, from an observor's point of view, what he is doing well or poorly. He does not associate much with deaf people and says that he is "pretty much fed up with them." He still becomes frustrated, but he is trying to work out the interpersonal dimension of the frustration in his own way. He feels that during the past few years, among the people who know about his disabilities, he has heard too much well-intended advice of what to do, when what he really needs is the time to figure those things out for himself.

He says, "I'm a long ways from being happy and satisfied, because I've got things I need to work on and I want to reach my goal. I still want to go back to college, but first I want to improve my English. I'd like to be able to explain some of the things I think about people. I know what I'm thinking and what I see, but I don't know how to explain it, because I don't have the right words. I don't know enough to be able to put it into sentences. But that's my goal, to explain what has happened to me and how I think and see things."

"I'm changing now and learning on my own how to deal with my frustrations. I'm trying to solve any problems right there when they happen, not wait until tomorrow. If it happens at work, say I bump into somebody, I'll explain what happened and let it go at that. Maybe he won't understand the first time, but maybe the second or third time he will. It depends on how good the other person is, how good an attitude he has. And it depends on me, how well I can help him and give him good information. I think we ourselves need to take responsibility to help other people understand. I think we need to learn to explain things and give other people a chance to give us a chance."

Hanna Berzinsh*

Hanna Ohmann Berzinsh was born in Moscow in 1907. She lived through early Bolshevik uprisings in Russia before returning with her family to their native Latvia in 1917. Some 20 years later, at the beginning of World War II, she endured Russian and then German invasion of her country, eventually fleeing with the German Army before yet another takeover by the Communists. She lived in eight German cities during the war, staying at refugee camps and working as a translator. After the Capitulation in 1945, she escaped to the American Zone of Berlin and waited 5 years to come to the United States. She has worked full time here from the year of her immigration until her recent mandatory retirement. Her English, the last of five languages she has mastered, is heavily accented and, grammatically, it often resembles her earlier tongues. Although she expresses herself through speech, she receives communication only through written notes. She has been partially hearing and partially sighted most of her life, the degrees of the impairments sometimes changing as the result of medical problems and treatments and, perhaps, from the trauma of her experiences.

"My father worked for Latvian Government. From start, we lived nice. Near Kremlin, we had nice apartment with

*The name has been changed.

maid. We went to park. But in 1914, that year is the start of the Revolution and my father was transferred to outside from Moscow. Russian soldiers were going house to house and shooting whom they did not likes. We had afraid what would happen in Moscow; we had to go somewhere less dangerous . . . better. Two years we lived there outside in suburb. I catch scarlet. In this time, they had not any good doctor−Revolution. I was sick about 3 months with scarlet. I was not born deaf, no. Then I catch diphtheria and I was sick more; I cannot go to school. I went to school before 1 or 2 years in Moscow, but that is all. In 1917, my mother died. In Russia, when one dies, the pastor must spray with holy water. But my mother did not have this done; we are Lutheran. They did not allow my mother to be buried in cemetery. Two weeks my mother's body was in apartment. We cannot bury; no one took her. We had no casket−in 1917 cannot find. My father ordered one man, he paid this man to pick up this body, somewhere to take it from our apartment. I don't know where she is buried. Maybe she is eaten. In these times, they eat horse, dog, cat−there is no food. I don't know. My father paid money to take it away.

"After mother died, my father lost his work and we applied for immigration to Latvia. We are Latvian nationals. We were still in the suburb and there was no train to Moscow. It was winter−snow, ice, sleet. Horse and cart bring my father, sister, and me. Horse for 2 weeks have no food to eat. And when we came to Moscow, our train was gone. We came too late and first refugee trains are gone. Father have one friend in Moscow and we stayed at friend's, waiting second train. After 2 months, we are told to go outside of Moscow for extra train. We went to this train and there are army men. We present our passports. This train was not for people, no. It was merchandise train. In middle of each car, here is a small oven, wood oven. We sleep on shelves . . . no mattress, no nothing.

"There were many, many come. When train was full, army men shut doors and told us to wait, next day we start. The train had no restroom, no couch. We went to sleep, but in the morning we didn't go. We waited 1, 2, 3 days; we could not get out. People banged on doors, but army men start to shoot. We have to stand still, no noises. But how long? We had nothing to eat, no water. It was 3 days now, we have no restroom there. We went to sleep and hear the train start to move. We stopped in the woods and we looked out-there was no more army. Some go out to restroom, some start to get food. Some men go out to cut wood for oven to melt snow for drinking. Train start moving and they are out. My father got back, but some were far away. They were left in the woods with the wolves. They never came back. It took 3 months to get to Latvia-2 days stop, 1 day move, 3 days stop, 1 day move. The train did not go with coal, but wood. And if this wood is all gone, the train must stop in the middle of the woods and the men go out chopping wood to start the train. We had about 75 wagons long. We had no food. Stomachs got big, faces sucked in. People got sick and infected with lice-3 months no wash.

"Come to Latvia, all must go to hospital. My father got some work in Latvia and we had there my aunt. After all these experiences, I start to go blind. Nobody knows why I start blind. I went to doctor, he told me from diphtheria, scarlet, and all these experiences in the train-the cold, eating not perfect food. I was then 10 years old. At start it goes slow. But later on, it gets worse, worse, worse and after about 1 year, total blind-I see nothing. They think the scarlet and diphtheria left something, and all those experiences.... They think it is something left in the nerves. In that year, 1917, there is not so good doctors as now. They gave me some medicine to drink and drops for my eyes. He told me I must drink real coffee extract. Terrible, terrible this coffee was... so thick. After 1 or 2 years, I start to see better. My father told me I had surgery... I don't remember. But I start to see again, maybe not so perfect, but I can see and read. Doctor warned, maybe I have in my head something different now with my nerves. He told me maybe I will have disease in my ears. But I was not thinking of this. I start school-I was happy. So happy! When I start school, four grades of school my hearing was good. But suddenly-doctor don't know why-I start hearing problem. My left ear was no good. I go to doctor and he say it is from otosclerosis. They told me I might start to lose everything. They give me medicine and that kept me until I finish high school. I must sit in first bench so I can better see and, when teacher talk, can better hear. But in this time I can still see good and have no hearing aid.

"In this time, my father is working again. He work in finance for government. We have big apartment—my father, my sister, me, and one maid—in Riga. Riga is capital of Latvia. We have also one big farm with horse, cow, nice big cherry garden, about 40 miles from town. We go there in summers and father comes on weekends. I went to school, 17 years. First I go 12 years and finish high school, and then to Academie. Father gave us money, plenty money, but he has no time to go with us. He come home at 11 from meeting, conference. My sister and I, after school, take off uniform, take off hat, stick in handbag and go out to restaurant, out for coffee, dancing all night. We had many, many friends. We go skating, horse riding in the stars, tennis playing. One time, I go to Estonia, I broke my leg ski jumping. Another time, I have a friend who is a doctor... he let me drive his sports car and I crash it up. Every year we have Christmas party—finish classes, we have ball. All classes go to Christmas party, we dance all night. Each 3 years, go to Carnival. One time I go as gypsy; one time dress up as clown. We had nice life. Maid cannot tell, 'Do this.' I think if I have mother, I cannot live like this. Mother say, 'Come home from school, study.' I had no mother. We are very happy no mother. We don't like if father married second time; we'd have stepmother, cannot go out. But maid... cannot say.

"I start Academie 1934, I am 27. I take languages, art, and some sport. When I start Academie, I think if I finish, I be painter. I have in school French, German, Latvian, and Esperanto. I know already Latvian, Russian, and German. My father's grandfather came to Latvia from Germany; we speak German and Latvian at home. In Moscow, maids speak Russian and I learn Russian. When I go to the Academie, I work at University of Latvia as typist.

"Nineteen thirty-nine, all okay. I work, go to school. I could hear, but hearing gets worse; eyes good. Russians come and nationalize. My father lost his work. My father give up farm and apartment before Russians pick up, but we don't get this money. We buy small house—father, sister, her husband and children, and me. Russians make me translator. All documents must be translated from Latvian to Russian. I work in Department of Agriculture for bookkeeping, typing, and translating. Before, in school, I was hard of hearing, but still hear plenty good. I got worse in 1939.

"Communists don't like people who have money. Russians sent to Siberia who have money, take everything. Massive deportation to Siberia start June 14. Many of my relatives, uncle and aunt, they take away. They come in night with big wagon. Knock on the door, come inside, they take you as you sleep. When start to hear of deportation, father no more sleep home for 1 or 2 months. In the day he come home, then go away. He sleep one night by this friend, one night by that friend. They come to my house, but they don't catch father. Literature, books, they all pick up. I feel afraid.

"One night I go to sleep . . . I dream I go on big ship and ship sank. I swim and I see one man. I tell him to come to me and this man comes. I say, 'How long have you been in the water?' He speaks something to me, but I do not hear him. I tell him, 'Speak louder.' And he says, 'There will come a time when you will be more happy deaf than hearing.' I say, 'No, no.' I wake up, put watch to my ear, I cannot hear it tick. I start to cry. I am mad at this man in my dream—I woke up hard of hearing. I hear little. People talk close, I can hear okay; far, no. Doctor says is from the Occupation and father not here . . . nerves. I still can hear, but not good.

"In 1940, the Germans came and occupied. Russians and Jews fly out to Russia. My father would like work, but Germans did not give back job. My father was upset. One night had heart attack and died from this heart attack. I work . . . translate all papers from Russian now to German. My boyfriend is captain in German Army, but he is married. Less than 1 year, we know the Russians will come back. Latvians thought Russians would pick up, take all good things to Russia. Germans tell me if I go to Germany, then companies will come back after war and we can live in Latvia. I know how terrible times are under Russians, so I go to Germany.

"I go in ship with German Army. Russians bomb ship and one piece separates, but ship didn't sink. Another ship went down and my ship picked up half the passengers. In Germany I live in refugee camps and translate papers—prisoner of war papers. Never spy, only prisoner of war. Each time the Russians come down and pick up, we move—Königsberg, Steten, Pires, Pasvalk, Rügen, Lübeck, Hamburg, Brandenburg. In Brandenburg, near Berlin, short before Capitulation I was in shelter in basement of hospital, translating. One night, bombs came over. I was in shelter 2 or 3 days before they came and dug me up. They took me to hospital. When I get my consciousness up, they tell me it is Russian Zone. I have afraid. Berlin is divided in four zones–American, French, British, Russian. In hospital they give me man's shoes–one big, one small. One night, I go out from hospital in these shoes and ask, 'Where is the American Zone?' And I walk. Not only me, there is about 50 people who walk ... so far. The Russian Army had different uniforms than American and when we see American uniforms we asked them to take us in. They told all of us they cannot keep us in Berlin. They don't know what Berlin will be, if it will be picked up, or how far it will be, which border. But I got paper from General Dwight Eisenhower. He wrote us all who like to fly from Communists, we go to Flemsburg. It is neutral town, not in the shooting, near Danish border. He told, it is German, but neutral. But if the Russians occupy Flemsburg, we must go over border to Denmark. Oh I was so happy. French all refugee send back, but United States and England no send back. I think, better to go to America. Here I have one aunt. I cannot go back to Latvia. Terrible with Communists.

"Before the bombs, I can hear little bit. But after that, lost entire. I cannot hear. From 1945 to 1951, I lived in refugee camps and worked there, in four camps. The last is Bremen. From Bremen camp I emigrate to U.S.A. Until last half-year, I translate and I make dolls for soldiers. For American and British soldiers, I make dolls in Latvian national costume and sell. Last, I was in transit camp. American official told me better to get married. Here in America I will from start have no job–deaf–if cannot find job, must be domestic, dishwasher. He said get married. I married one Latvian who was in camp. He was lawyer, 7 years younger than me. I know him from dances and parties in camp, but I did not want to marry him. But I marry and live with him 5 months. I pass all medical exams and got visa. My husband got visa. Last we must swear to consulate inspector we did not shoot any Americans, were not jailed, were not in Communist or Nazi organizations. I swore, but my husband no swear. He said, 'I will not emigrate to U.S.A.' I had 1 year more in transit camp. I learn more English and they teach me how to repair clothes. Catholic Welfare Council guaranteed $1,000; I am deaf, so when I come here I will have a little money. All this time, I learn English. Before, when I translate prisoner of war papers, I learn a little from dictionary. Now I know I will go to America, I study more from dictionary. I have dictionary with Latvian, English, French, German, Russian. We go on big ship, 3,000 refugees come here. Because I am deaf, I have paper... do not have to work on ship. I can work, ja, but this work I do not like-many were seasick and women must clean up. I not tell them I can work. I swim, some warm days lie in sun, study English. Ship come to New York for Thanksgiving, November 24, 1951. I was 44 years old.

"Ship comes to New York and I see Statue of Liberty. They bring us Thanksgiving eating to ship. Go before doctor and have shots. I send telegram from immigration to my aunt in Washington. We stay 3 days on ship, then I go to my aunt in Maryland suburb. Her husband came before through Seventh Day Adventist Church. They give him job in hospital. I stayed 3 months with my aunt, but there were too many-aunt, uncle, cousin, me-with only one bedroom. I sleep on couch. I see ad in drugstore for domestic work, and I go clean people's house, iron. Then rent room in basement in Maryland for $25 a month-with bed, table, and chair. No kitchen; bathroom share three. And I work to clean house. I do not use this money from National Catholic Welfare Council. But I do not like this work. Latvian pastor in Maryland help me to find Goodwill Industries. After 6 months I apply for Goodwill and they give me work. I live in Maryland in this room for 2 years and take two buses to Goodwill. But it is too much riding back and forth by bus. So I move to Washington to one small room near Georgetown for $48 per month. Goodwill pays me only 50 cents per hour, but now I don't need bus. I can walk to work. This apartment is efficiency, but I do not like to cook. In Latvia, sometimes the maid told us, will teach us to cook-if marry, need to know how to cook. We say, 'Go to hell.' When I come here, I have no time to cook; eat in cafeteria. I work at Goodwill fixing dresses, zippers, sewing buttons. Two times I was on television to demonstrate how in Europe they repair clothes. Goodwill gets lots of money from these television commercials.

"When I come here I go to Latvian Church. I go, but I don't hear what they say. Here in Washington are about 400

Latvians, no more. All is married, have children, not interested to be with me. Sometimes I go to Catholic cathedral, but nothing hear. No one talks to me. They talk, talk, talk. I cannot hear. And I cannot see good to lipread—image is not that clear. I can see only a few inches clearly. I lipread in Latvia, but here I have too hard see and I am total deaf. Sometimes Latvians have at church a bazaar, this and that, and I go, but I can't hear. What I do? At church many people like talk, and I sit. No one talk to me. I don't have a friend at church. Not for me.

"I had one friend; she was from Latvia. She had brain tumor—hard see from brain tumor. I meet her in my church in Maryland or at Goodwill, I cannot remember which first time. She was one and I was one. One alone and one alone, we start talking. I didn't know her in Latvia. Sometimes we went downtown, to a park, to a restaurant. When I was at Goodwill a friend come to visit me from Norway in 1956. I know her from Germany. I know another family from Germany, I went one time to Philadelphia for visit. This woman, she worked in Goodwill 3 months. Her hip has shrapnel from bomb and she had operation for a metal pin so she can walk. Her husband work in Washington for U.N., but when U.N. moves to Brussells, he was laid off. They move to Philadelphia.

"I go one time to see my friends from Latvia. In New York. I sleep one night in their house, then in the morning go out alone. I go to Empire State Building. I go down, in subway, and drive around; I come out and I am lost. I go to policeman and say, 'Please help me. I am lost in New York.' He ask from what country I come. I tell him, 'Washington, D.C.' He say, 'Good; come.' He take me to police house. I tell him I am deaf—I cannot hear. He ask me from what area is my friend's house. I say, 'Second Street.' He say, 'Ja, but from Manhattan, Brooklyn, Queens. . .?' I say 'I don't know . . . only Second Street.' So I waited until he finish work and the policeman told me, if I am not afraid of him, he will take me in the night to find my Second Street house. But I told him, 'New York is so big, how can find?' He say will find. We drive all night. All together 18 hours I wait and eat, and driving . . . but we find the house. It was very nice adventure; first in U.S.A.

"I worked still for Goodwill, but I see this work is not for me. I don't like this sewing; secretary, typing, translating—those I like. And my salary is only 50 cents an hour. So I start to go to school for better job. Here, if you are handicapped–deaf–you cannot find work. Must have school papers. I have school papers, but in Latvia. So I start to go to school for keypunch and speedtype certificate and learn English to get citizenship. If I don't have citizenship, I can't have office job. I go to Temple School. The classes are $14 a lesson, so I can go only sometimes, once a week. Sometimes I am not eating, but I go to school. At night and on weekend, I study and learn American history for citizenship. I learn from book and when I go to court, they use paper. There were 32 questions and I was so nervous because I like to get citizenship. But I have only two wrong. I got citizenship April 9, 1957. I get citizenship and I have paper from school, so I start to look for better work.

"I take Civil Service and they classify me as clerk typist and keypunch. I am deaf, but I have this–I pass test. But Civil Service is long list; must wait and wait until name comes to top. I cannot wait. I go to Library of Congress; they have work, ja, but I must lipread. I cannot lipread, but they send me to Washington Hearing Society. We sit in circle, but I cannot see to lipread. I cannot work in Library of Congress. So a lady at Goodwill says she can help me get new job. Work at Goodwill 5 years, I get job, and I leave Goodwill.

"I start to work for keypunch company in suburbs in 1957. In 1958, I have surgery first time on right eye for glaucoma. I lost my sight, went blind–one eye. When I start work, I applied to get car, but cop says no–eyes bad. I got permit, but the police told me I cannot drive, only in daylight. But to work, I get up in morning, go about 30 miles, come home at night–cannot have daylight. So each morning, wake up at 5, take city bus to Greyhound station, take Greyhound bus, ride to suburb. One lady from my company I pay to pick me up from highway, bring to work, at 5 bring back to highway for Greyhound bus. It takes 14 hours–8 hour work, 3 hours and 3 hours. If I miss bus in Washington, I cannot get Greyhound bus until 2 in the afternoon; too far to walk to company. So I move to new apartment near Greyhound station; can walk to bus and home. I still get up 5, come home 7. One time, one morning snow and bus broke, I must be at work. I promise to be–I no finish work and I told them I finish tomorrow. So, I take taxi to work, cost $12.50. When I move to this new apartment, store fix up light for doorbell.

"In 1963, I go in hospital again for eye surgery–10, 12 days. After glaucoma, I changed to another, better doctor and he told me for glaucoma wrong surgery, done wrong. And he told me left eye start cataract. In 1969, he does surgery on my eye, but no stitch. He told me if stitch it can get infection and I can get glaucoma. He give me cataract lens. My glasses is cataract lens. If I have no glasses, I can't see–oh, I can see you a little–here is person, here is light, here is something white. And I see half of you, half of you, half more. It is blurry and I see double, triple. With glasses, is a little blurry, but I can see. Can read, only close; but far away I can see better. I see good street–red, green light. Not so far sideways. I see sideways, but not far. If I need to look somewhere, I must turn my head. Must turn head, must look down to walk. I always look down, see curb. But in dark harder. I no see clear–all blurry. At night, come from working, hard see–all black. I wait at corner... other person crosses, I cross. One time I went in hospital for ears. They try to put something inside, maybe can hear better, but they must take out. So bad noise I cannot work. I have, also, hearing aid. But too much noise with typing–loud, loud noise. I don't like, I cannot think. I don't use.

"Six times I am robbed. Once in apartment and five times on street. In 1970, I come home from hospital, open door, oh, I screamed. Rings gone, bracelet, money. All is thrown here, here, here. I was afraid maybe person still inside. The manager come and call the police. They take fingerprint. Last time, in 1972–December 12, 1972 at 3:25–I come home from buying downtown Christmas presents for my co-workers. One man comes to me in front of park and I say 'Go,' and I start to walk. He hides in the bushes and he comes back. I call for help and he hit me in the shoulder and I lost consciousness. After he hit me I fall. I get up in George Washington Hospital and I have my shoulder broken in two places. After 2 weeks I can go home. My co-workers send me this Christmas tree on my table, all filled with money–$1, $5, $10–all together $185. They send me all these animals, too, each time I am in hospital, and for Christmas, my birthday. They know I like animals. And that time, in hospital, they send a card with all names–70 names. Doctor in hospital asked how I can remember so many people. I know them all–not work in same room, but in same company. But not friends–co-workers. Only two ever come here.

"Across street from work is government building. We have at work cafeteria with vending machines, but most of the people don't like. They go to eat somewhere else–we have lunchtime, 1 hour. They go across the street to cafeteria or to a restaurant. My co-workers sometimes say, 'Come,' another time, another says, 'Come eat.' I know that to lipread . . . fast, fast, fast, put on my coat, I go. If someone ask, I go. If no one ask, I go to cafeteria from machines.

"When I work keypunching I have a long time my friend from Latvia with brain tumor. We go sometimes together. Alone, too, in the summer, Saturday, Sunday, I go to park–feed birds, feed squirrels. But in winter, 7 or 8 months I work Saturdays overtime. Five or six times I work Sundays; but Saturday, many times all day. But when I am 65 I must retire. I was first who retire in company's history so they give me party. We have more than 1500 employees. Four hundred come to party. I don't know all the names, but the faces, ja. My boss pinned me orchid. I started to cry, but he said 'Don't cry.' I have picture of friends from my work, my co-workers. At 65 lay off; they hire me back part time. In 1972, layoff; 1973, I work 5 months; 1974, I work 5 or 6 months. In 1975, company install TV screen that sends sound signals for errors. The machine whines–I cannot hear. Company not ask me back for part time."

"Now I have only Social Security, no pension. When I start work, they told me when I finished, they would pay me pension. But after company is merged twice, they told me I have not 12 years work. I work 14 years–9 years and 3 years and 2 years–but they told me they cannot pay pension; must work one company 12 years. So I get Social Security–$250 a month, half of my month's salary.

"Sometimes, I worked more. I work overtime many times. I have no family, no friends. I am deaf, I have no friends here–no boyfriends, no girl friends. I am alone. I had my Latvian girl friend, but she died of a brain tumor 5 years ago. I had friends in Latvia, in Germany, but America, none. At my work, all the people are young, married, with children. They cannot be friends. And so far away—there was no one from Washington. I had many friends when I was in Europe. I was not deaf. But now I am deaf and old, no one likes me.

"A woman at my work is deaf and dumb, she no speak. Sometimes she comes to pick up her husband at *Washington Post*, a few blocks from my apartment. She comes sometimes first to me. We go downtown to wait until he finish work. But I don't know when she comes. She comes and if I am here, we go downtown. One time her husband work all night, she slept here in the same bed. Her husband was on strike but *Post* start to hire new people. He had afraid would lose job—he is also deaf-dumb—so he go back to work. But he told me not to buy *Post* anymore. He said, 'Publisher K. Graham is millionaire but she will not pay good salary.' Man must feed sometimes six children on this little salary, so I start to buy *Star*.

"I belong to the Samaritan Club. I go two or three times a month. Saturday they pick up me. They come, put note under my door, coming tomorrow, and I wait. They have about nine people, all total blind. I am only one who is deaf. They talk, talk, talk. We go to park, to Botanic Garden where there is Braille. About 3 hours on Saturday. I go with people, but not friends. I see my aunt one time per 3 months, maybe, when she sends me letter. If I have good feeling, I go there. If no good feeling, I don't go. Christmas, Easter... I do nothing. Sometimes go to church. My aunt take me to her house, I eat lunch. My cousin is biochemist; her husband is architect. They take me to the bus and I come back. But if I no go to church, then nothing. I go to park, feed squirrels.

"Every day in morning, if it's nice, I pick up squirrel nuts and go to park. Here is nearby six parks. I feed squirrels each day one park... stay 4 hours. If it's cold or rain, 3 hours. It is too lonely to sit in house all day. Summer, I pick up apple or lunch, stay park all day. Sit on bench, read book. Squirrel comes to bench to pick up nuts. They come to my bench, smell my shoes... slow, slow, come to bench, pick up peanut from my pocket, sometimes from handbag, and run. Sometimes come back. If I don't pick up lunch, then sit in park, go eat in Harrington Hall or Sholl's Cafeteria. Go back and sit in park until it's dark, then come home. Come home, do needlepoint, read book. I like scientific mystery book—like

F.B.I., real stories, what some people's experiences are in life, not fiction. I read Russian, Latvian, German, English. I have some foreign books, but hard to find German, Russian. Here in store is some magazine but there is only sexy girl. I don't like it. I like more that I can think about. I read newspaper, foreign politic, but I don't like how is written. All denounce one another–this no good, this no good; I like to read foreign politic from outside America–France's election or Italy or Middle East, but foreign papers hard to find. Only girls dancing–trash. I have no TV, I don't like TV. TV shoot, kill, hit. I live in Germany when bombs came in Second World War. I lived under this war–hell–from 1939 to 1945. TV is also many violence–no!

"Sometimes before when I go to park in the summer, I took some needlepoint. But some women come around, looking... stop, sit down... 'What do you do, I like to see that.' But I no hear, I don't like. I don't like if people know I am deaf. I don't like writing note if I go to cafeteria; some look at me, I don't like. Maybe if born deaf, ja, but I no born deaf. In school I don't like teacher say, 'Sit here.' Some kids say 'Ha, ha, ha'; I don't like. At work, not all know I am deaf. Maybe upstairs, some don't know. Here, sometimes, when I go to cafeteria, some like to talk. I get up and go out. I don't like to tell him I am deaf. Maybe I am wrong, but I feel this. I am ashamed I am deaf. If I go to church or to club, people talk and laugh. I sit in corner, I cannot hear. I like to hear. Maybe if I were born deaf, that is different. Now I withdraw myself from the company of people. I don't like if they know I am deaf.

"I go to museums, White House, Capitol. In White House, gone five times. I see Eisenhower, Kennedy when they die; I see Humphrey at the Rotunda. Sometimes sit at Washington Monument, feed squirrels. If I sit, don't know what to do, no good feeling... I go inside. About two, three times a month I go to National Geographic Society. They have movies; no buy, go free. Sometimes from Africa, from Sweden, or Eskimoes. I sit far away, last row; can see movie. Color I can see good far away, but black and white, blurry.

"I would like to go to Kennedy Center but I cannot go, no friends. Here were 'Figaro,' from Germany. I ask this lady I know downstairs to come with me, but she says she don't like opera. She nothing like. She have three or four friends, go only with her friends. When I think of music I cry. I love music. I really love music. If I hold a radio to my ear, I can hear little bit. In Latvia, I went to opera, the second nights–'Carmen', 'Othello', 'Rigoletto,' 'Madame Butterfly.' I'd like to go to Kennedy Center, see ballet, or movie. I like to be more free. Deaf-blind keep me by here. I cannot be free. Maybe if I have one friend who two times a week can go with me downtown, to restaurant, to park, can go with me to Kennedy Center, then I be more free. But now I am one; I have afraid to go in the dark night. Cop told me not go out one alone at night. Two is all right, but not one. I can pick up taxi, but I don't know who taxi man is.

"If I have a friend who is so free and likes traveling, I like to go somewhere to see more of U.S.A. or Canada or go to Europe or Arab country. I have no friends. I can't go one, deaf and part blind. Doctor told me not to leave alone. I have one eye, with cataracts. He told me I cannot sit down fast. If I fall on the floor suddenly I might lose my eye–no stitches in eye. After last surgery, doctor told me he operate but no stitch. He told me if they put in stitch they might hurt eye, might get glaucoma anyway. He told me if I have sudden fall or rough push, I might lose my eyesight. So I must be careful not to fall down. He told me I no travel one–I might lose my sight and if I go so far away how I can come back if I no see and hear? If here I go to park, I can tell man where my home or my aunt. But if I go to Canada or Europe, I no can come back.

"I am member Animal Protection Club. Sometimes they send paper to get signatures for some Congressmen ... to stop lay trap or poisoning in federal lands. I sign. Sometimes they send to Canada to Trudeau. In the traps, animal is stuck; he cannot get out. Sometimes get sheep, not only wolf or fox. They can trap, ja, but they must go looking. But they no look and animals die ... for 2 or 3 months cannot get food to eat. I march with Animal Protection Club by Canadian Embassy to stop killing seals. Three times I march– Canadian Embassy, Russian Embassy, Australian Embassy. When President Carter told human rights, we went to Russian Embassy ... Latvian group. We march by Russian Embassy and burn Russian flag. Latvian organization send letter to all Latvians, go march. We ask why they didn't let friends and family visit here. We went to protest. By Russian Embassy we have 25 marcher. Come by about 20 police in wagon to pick us up if we will not disperse in time. We all disperse, but there are more cops as protestors! And I march by Australian. Australian recognize Latvia as U.S.S.R.; America, no. We march there all day.

"My sister is married, three children in Latvia. Before she is married she went to college to be missionary. Learn many languages. In Latvia, she no work for army; I work for army as translator, but she have children, she no work outside. When I went to Germany, the Russian pick up our house. Now my sister live in four room apartment with seven families. That is no way to live. I send boxes–food, shoes, dress to my sister. I send each year three boxes; they have nothing. I have about 150 relatives in Latvia, but my close family, about seven–my sister, her children, grandchildren. If I send one, they all want. So when I send, I send each person one piece–one has dress, one has jacket, one gets gloves. Russian charge big duty, $160, $200. I send package last week, cost $638 duty only. To buy and send, all total cost $2,000. My cousin pick me up Sunday, I sleep their house in Maryland; Monday drive to Baltimore to harbor to send.

"I send to Appalachia. When I work, I must buy dresses, different dresses so wear same dress only once every 2 week. I retire, I have here 50 dresses. I don't need so many. I read in newspaper, poor people in Appalachia need some help. I ask lady downstairs to call for me to Appalachia. She call, man come here to pick up. One month before Christmas pick up two time. I find Lamb Foundation. Little children have no shoes, no clothes for snow. So I start to send money and my dresses. I have 11 boxes to send last November. I send to Appalachia many times, about 10. I send one time per year, my dresses or money.

"Now I have class Gallaudet College. I take pottery and fingerspelling. I like to learn sign language, but people sign so fast, I cannot understand. And if I go to cafeteria and start to sign, they think I'm crazy. I must do a,b,c; I like to fingerspell better. If I go blind, I cannot see signs, but finger–can hold hand, read word. And pottery, I like pottery. But these classes is just six times, four times, not every week. Man come, pick me up and drive me to Gallaudet College. Now I have three classes, fingerspelling on Monday, arts and crafts on Tuesday, and pottery on Thursday. Sometimes, class is cancelled, I cannot know. I go downstairs, wait and wait, from 6 to 8:30. So I tell them, this lady downstairs, they can call her and she will write me note, put under my door. Sometimes class cancelled because of snow, teacher sick, not many classes. I never miss class; I ready, I wait ... but class misses me! I like to read. If I were not deaf, I like to take class in psychiatry, mental medicine, not surgery. I like to know why people are mental sick. Why people spy? What this one is thinking? I like to know why a person is not normal. I must ask him his life and combine. What I like is to combine something. Why he Communist? Why he Nazi? I like work with brain.

"When I was lay off, I go to Red Cross volunteers. But I cannot help. They say work with children or old people. I cannot–I cannot hear. I like to help with old people in hospital, help from bed, but I cannot; I don't have the strength. I like to make for doctors stick with cotton tips, but they have 10 people do that; that is all. I like to do office, but they have none. Work with blind, I try, ja, go two places. But I cannot hear. They have no volunteer work for deaf people. I don't want to sit home all day. I'm tired of it. I am too nervous. I go out to park, see people. If I were not blind and deaf, I would not work as keypunch. I could go to store as salesgirl. Salesgirl can be 80 years old. I go ask ... be cashier. But no, I cannot hear. Now, if I work part time, lose Social Security, Medicare. Then I must pay high insurance. I pay already Blue Cross. More I cannot pay. Nothing can do now. No friends, no work. I do here needlepoint. For whom? I can nothing plan. If I have some friends, we can go somewhere. I have no one. Go to park, feed squirrel.

"I like to have some work. If I can find some work I don't need to thinking. I must look at what I do. But sit all day and nothing do.... Work or some friends–that is my two dreams. Work or friends. Then I will be free. Now I have nothing to do–twiddle my thumbs. I do not need money. Before I work overtime. Social Security is $250, room is $105; $145 left. For food is enough; clothes I don't need. I have money in bank for burial; I have cemetery plot at Rock Green Cemetery, a place where to sleep. Before every Saturday, have shampoo and set hair. Now go two or three times per year if I go somewhere. If I had friends, go out, I would have tint. But who sees? I better to spend money for squirrel nuts, my friends in the park. They come to pick up from my pockets. They are my friends."

Mary Barker Boyd*

Mary Barker Boyd, a 64-year-old woman, has lived with deaf-blindness most of her life. Born deaf, her own total blindness did not occur until she was in her thirties, although she had experienced night blindness from the time she was 8 years old. Two of her three older sisters have also been deaf-blind. Agnes was 13 years older than Mrs. Boyd and Helen, 10 years older; both had developed night blindness and tunnel vision while Mrs. Boyd was still a young child. When Mrs. Boyd—as she always refers to herself—left the family homestead 18 years ago, she married a man, then 61, who had been totally deaf and totally blind for 42 years.

Mrs. Boyd was born and reared in rural Tennessee. Her parents owned two tobacco farms, one of which they tended for their livelihood. She was the youngest of eight children. Her four older brothers, she says, were "normal." The four girls, however, all seem to have had congenital abnormalities. Louise, the second youngest child, was blind in one eye and feeble-minded. An assessment of symptoms strongly suggests that the other three sisters all had Usher's Syndrome. Each of them was born deaf (Mrs. Boyd says that Agnes became deaf as an infant; more likely, since she was the first deaf child in the family, her hearing loss was not immediately discovered); each developed night blindness

*Names of people and places have been changed, including cities, states, and state schools.

during childhood; each, as a teenager and young woman, exhibited the stumbling and colliding associated with a loss of peripheral vision, although Mrs. Boyd, at least, does not remember the specific "tunneling-in" as her sight slowly and steadily declined.

Nor is Mrs. Boyd aware of the genetic condition called Usher's Syndrome. She and her sisters have long attributed their blindness to accidental causes. "Agnes lost her vision after measles. Measles reduced her vision and then she could see less and less and less. Helen became blind at night from chicken pox when she was 11 or 12. She could still see during the day until an accident with cologne. She misunderstood how to use cologne and sprayed some in her face. It got in her eyes and she became totally blind. I could see all right until I was 7 years old. We had a coal heater. You pour kerosine oil over the wood logs and coal to make the fire start quickly. I poured some kerosine on the fire and it flared up! Flames burst from the coal heater and burned my hair and face. It ruined my eyes; I could no longer see at night. But I could see during the day until I was 32. I was at a deaf party. They asked me to stand up in front of a movie camera and sign stories. There were six powerful lights in front of me. I looked up and everything was red. I went outside and I couldn't see. I thought I was losing my vision. I told my brother Ralph and he took me to a doctor. The doctor said the nerves in my eyes had died."

Despite these suppositions, Mrs. Boyd has realized that the strong incidence of deaf-blindness in her family may be more than simply coincidental. Her ultimate explanation of the deaf-blindness and Louise's limited intellectual capacity is a kind of "folk genetics"–"four girls gave my mother bad luck." She recalls, however, that at her wedding, the minister asked her brother Chester how it happened that three of his sisters were deaf-blind. Chester replied that his parents were cousins.

Mrs. Boyd attended the Tennessee School for the Deaf from ages 8 to 15. She still advocates the school's philosophy of the twenties with regard to teaching English to deaf children–that fingerspelling entire sentences, not signing, should be used in all communication. Today, her English is very good, probably due not only to instruction, but also to an early introduction to language by her older deaf sisters, and constant reading in Braille during her later life. Although she does not speak, she seems to have no difficulty communicating with hearing people. If they do not know sign language or fingerspelling, she prints in their palms.

Mrs. Boyd remembers little from her school years. In the sixth grade, her final year, she was no longer allowed to play on intramural sports teams, for her vision was poor and she was frequently hit in the face by flying balls. "The school did not want to be responsible if I got hurt." She does not know why she started school so late; the reason for her premature departure, however, was the Depression. Her father had died during the twenties. One older brother had been killed in an accident and the others were married with their own families to support. When her mother could no longer provide her with travel money for school vacations, or her school clothing and activity fees, Mrs. Boyd returned home. Agnes and Helen had already left school without graduating because of poor vision and problems with other deaf children teasing them. Mrs. Boyd wonders why they had not been sent to the state school for the blind, but she assumes, with her typical faith in the present day, that 50 years ago educators did not know how to help a child with the dual loss.

Without her sons, Mrs. Boyd's aging mother found it impossible to work the farm. Earlier, when Mrs. Boyd had lived at home, and on her school vacations, she had worked in the fields, separating tobacco leaves from their stems. She had also enabled Agnes to work by guiding her around the "stones, stumps, and plows." In the early thirties, however, her mother rented out the farm and their large farmhouse and moved with her four daughters to a smaller house down the road.

For the next 12 years, Mrs. Boyd was, like her mother, "on vacation,"-and, in fact, she has never worked outside of her own home. To improve her English, she studied a dictionary; she helped her mother around the house and yard and worked in their small garden; she learned to cook and enjoyed sewing. In addition, she had her mother and sisters for company. "All my life Agnes was my 'pal' sister. Not Helen-she had a hot temper. But Agnes and I were like a happily married couple. We never fought." Mrs. Boyd guided Agnes to church in town every Sunday, a long trip requiring Greyhound bus service. By that time Agnes must have been totally blind and Helen nearly so. Helen had married when Mrs. Boyd was in school, but because of financial and transportation problems, she lived at home and her husband stayed with her only on weekends.

Mrs. Boyd says she did not marry when she was young because she did not have the opportunity to meet deaf men. "We were poor. If I had money to travel around, maybe I would have met a deaf man in Tennessee or Kentucky, but there were not many people where we lived. Helen's husband was not a smart man. One Navy man wanted to marry me, but my mother said, 'Don't marry a hearing man. If deaf and hearing marry, later there may be trouble and you will have to divorce.'"

When Mrs. Boyd was 28, her mother died and the sisters moved together to a small house on their farm property. Ralph gave them small amounts of money for essential purchases–food and clothing–and handled their utility bills. Mrs. Boyd's eyesight must have been severely restricted by this time, for Louise, the feeble-minded sister, had to assume the role of mother to her sisters for all activities away from the house. She accompanied them on shopping excursions to town and guided them to the mailbox at the tenant farmer's house. Although Louise could not read, she sometimes transliterated printed letters into fingerspelling and thus communicated her sisters' mail to them. They preferred to visit with the farmer's wife and have her palm-print her letters to them. They also brought her pails of garbage as slop for her pigs.

In the operation of their home, the deaf-blind sisters were largely independent. Agnes did the cooking, but they all shared the housework. With no modern appliances, they spent a considerable amount of time doing their chores. By the time she was in her early thirties, a few years after her mother's death, Mrs. Boyd could no longer see at all. She does not remember feeling depressed or upset. She says simply, "I felt sorry that I couldn't read the newspaper and books. I felt sorry, but I didn't cry. I was calm." She indicates, too, that with her sisters' presence and many relatives frequently dropping by, she felt neither deprived of social relationships nor lonely.

Ten years passed until, when Mrs. Boyd was 44, Louise died. Louise had been responsible for lighting the fire in the coal heater each morning. Often, when she leaned over the heater, the sweater pocket in which she kept her matches touched the hot coals and caught on fire. Mrs. Boyd says, "I told her to stop all the time. 'It's dangerous for you. Don't keep matches in your sweater.' But she couldn't think. On April 1st, 1958, we were all awake. Agnes and I were cooking breakfast. I had a headache. I got an aspirin and lay down. I was on my bed, but I felt Louise jump and shake. The whole house shook. I went downstairs and I smelled burnt clothes. I was frightened. I felt all around-where are the clothes burning? I was searching, touching everything. I found Louise. 'What happened?' She answered it was the fire. The tenant farmer came over and said she might not live. She was badly burned. She couldn't talk; her nerves were shocked. But she could still sign a little bit. I was very frightened. An ambulance came and brought her to town. We waited. She lived from 8 o'clock to 5:30, then she died."

"Then we were stuck-helpless. She had helped and helped until she died. Then we had no one to help us. We were forced to stay home all the time. We just stayed in the yard close to the house. Sometimes Agnes and I tried to find the way to the farmer's house, but we could not. We tripped on the embankment and walked the wrong way, but the farmer's wife saw us and brought us home. There were snakes around that could bite us. My brother said, 'Don't go far; just stay at home.'"

The restriction made that an unpleasant period for Mrs. Boyd, but it was relatively brief. Two years later, a friend-another deaf-blind woman-visited from Alabama. She knew a deaf-blind man who wanted to find a wife. She told the three sisters about Mr. James Boyd who lived in Florida. Mr. Boyd was just 60 years old. He had lost his hearing from scarlet fever when he was 2 years old; his vision had slowly declined until he became blind at 19. For more then 30 years he had caned chairs, then made mops at the workshop for the blind in his hometown. For 20 years he had lived independently in a boarding house near his job. His parents had been dead for a decade and his sisters and deaf friends were aging. Mr. Boyd thought that he would be happier if he married; he did not want to be lonesome as he grew old.

All three sisters were interested in Mr. Boyd and the prospect of marriage. He and Agnes, both of whom knew

Braille, began to exchange letters. She described her family and invited him to come to Tennessee. He made the trip during his Fourth of July holiday; their brother, Chester, met him at the bus station and drove him to the farm. His purpose in visiting was to decide which sister to marry. He wanted a wife who could cook, a prerequisite that disqualified Helen. (Helen's husband and two brothers, Ralph and John, had all died during the fifties.) Mr. Boyd liked both Agnes and his future wife, but Agnes told him that she was old (like him, 60) and not in good health; she might die before too long. She suggested that he marry her younger sister. Mr. Boyd was agreeable, but he wanted his future wife first to learn Braille, and he asked Agnes to teach her. With tentative plans to marry the following year, he returned to Florida.

Mrs. Boyd applied herself assiduously to the study of Braille. A sister-in-law secured lessons for her through the correspondence courses program of the Hadley School for the Blind in Winnetka, Illinois. In 4 months, Mrs. Price learned to read Braille. Agnes then tutored her in writing it manually with a slate and stylus. They notified Mr. Boyd that she was ready and he came for a longer visit at Christmas time in order to make wedding plans.

Mrs. Boyd says that her wedding was an event of interest in her area. In addition to the many relatives who attended—nieces, nephews, and their children—people in nearby towns were curious about the marriage of a deaf-blind couple and, though uninvited, appeared at the wedding. It was held in the sisters' home, for Mr. Boyd's income was small. He and Mrs. Boyd agreed that it would be wiser to save their money rather than to rent the church. Reverend William Beckham, a deaf man who had been Mr. Boyd's classmate at the Florida School for the Deaf and who had, for 40 years, remained a close friend despite their living 300 miles apart, drove Mr. Boyd to Tennessee and conducted the wedding ceremony. Mrs. Boyd says that she was very, very happy to marry and has loved her husband, a "very good man," ever since. After the service, Reverend Beckham drove the couple back to Mr. Boyd's hometown and helped them settle into the apartment he had found for them.

The Boyds lived in near poverty for the first 3 years of

their marriage. Initially, they subsisted on Mr. Boyd's salary of $32 a week. That was in the early 1960's. Although their rent was small–$12 a week–his income was not adequate for them to live properly. Unable to afford meat or vegetables, they ate starches. Twice, Reverend Beckham found them new apartments after he discovered moths and roaches in their flour bins and lard, but they remained in a poor neighborhood. Their apartments had to be within walking distance to the workshop for the blind because they could not afford daily bus fare for Mr. Boyd. Mrs. Boyd says she once asked her husband's former vocational rehabilitation counselor (Mr. Boyd had not been on an active caseload since he had started working at the workshop) if she, too, could be employed at the workshop, but he told her that couples could not work together. He says now that they must have misunderstood each other since that has never been the workshop's policy.

After a year or 2, Mr. Boyd's hours were reduced because the workshop had more mops than it could sell. His pay check reflected his shorter workweek; he began to bring home only $24, then $22. Mrs. Boyd approached his supervisor for help in finding more money. The man referred her to the city's welfare office, downtown in the courthouse building, and the Boyds found their way there themselves.

(Mr. Boyd knows his city well. All the years that he had lived alone, he had been a familiar figure on the streets, raising his cane to alert oncoming cars that he intended to cross at an intersection. Witnesses say that cars often screeched to a halt as he, oblivious to the traffic, made his way across the street.

When Mrs. Boyd moved to town, her husband's sister offered to do their grocery shopping and help with other chores, but Mrs. Boyd declined her assistance. She says that her husband taught her the routes that she needed to know, and from the beginning she had no trouble navigating or finding store managers to help her. When asked about difficulties in adjusting to her new city and new homes, Mrs. Boyd says only that she was frightened of her gas stove and had to be patient and pray that she would learn to use it correctly. Other people, however, remember differently. The former vocational rehabilitation counselor recalls, for example, that they had terrible difficulty finding someone to help with shopping.

Now, almost 20 years later, the Boyds are well known to the storekeepers and taxicab drivers in their city. Earlier, however, Mrs. Boyd must have entered buildings and wandered or waited until someone realized that she was not only blind–with her dark glasses and cane, it is a very obvious disability–but also deaf. Once someone approaches and touches her, however, Mrs. Boyd has never been shy about taking the person's hand and writing in his palm, or extracting a piece of paper from her purse and writing a note explaining what she needs.)

After they entered the courthouse and were directed to the welfare office, the Boyds learned that they needed testimony from physicians that their deafness and blindness could not be reversed by surgery. Again, with Reverend Beckham's aid–Mrs. Boyd is also not bashful about sending letters to friends asking for help–they had their medical examinations and interviews with welfare personnel. In 1963, they were each awarded $46 a month in welfare payments, bringing their combined total income to $200 monthly. Shortly afterward, Reverend Beckham found them an unfurnished apartment, for Mrs. Boyd wanted her own furniture. With new monthly furniture bills to pay, the increase in income did not substantially improve their standard of living.

In 1964, however, a benefactor entered their lives. Joe Chicca was a businessman from New York. His firm had an office in the Boyd's city and he worked there for several months each year. One October, when he was downtown watching the Columbus Day Parade, he saw a blind man feeling a department store window for vibrations as the procession passed on the street. Joe was accustomed to helping disabled and poor people; there were many people in the two cities where he lived whom he regularly aided with money and more personal involvement. He approached Mr. Boyd to ask if he would like a ride home. Mr. Boyd must have indicated that Joe could write in his palm to communicate, but he refused the ride; both he and his wife are extremely cautious about entering cars with strangers. Later in the year, Joe saw Mr. Boyd rushing to work in the rain, and followed him to the workshop. He asked about the Boyds and learned that they still lived in an unpleasant apartment and still were not comfortable financially.

Joe changed their lives in many ways. For at least a year, Mrs. Boyd had been sending letters to a federally-supported housing project established for people with limited incomes. Repeatedly her applications were accepted, and replies were sent instructing her to make an appointment within a certain amount of time to sign a lease. With Mr. Boyd's sister frequently out of town nursing their very ill younger sister, and Reverend Beckham several hundred miles away, the Boyds had no one to read their printed mail to them regularly; the time deadline invariably was passed before Mrs. Boyd even knew that she had been accepted for the low-cost housing.

Joe arranged for the Boyds to move into one of the housing units. He paid their moving expenses and bought wall-to-wall carpeting and additional furniture for their home. He also bought two wrought-iron chairs that he had bolted to the sidewalk in front of their house. When the Boyds sit out in their chairs, bus drivers now realize that they are waiting for transportation and do not pass them by. Joe either arranged for the Boyds to be given a unit by a bus stop, or requested that the bus company establish a new stop there.

Joe persuaded Mr. Boyd to retire from his job when he reached 65, and he paid off their outstanding furniture bill. He also introduced other people into their lives, year-round residents of the community who could help them directly when Joe was in New York. One young woman, whom he was either helping with her own expenses or whom he paid for the service, visited the Boyds weekly to read them their mail. During the 9 months each year when he was in New York, Joe frequently sent her checks in her own name to cash for the Boyds. She says that she did so and, on her own initiative, always had Mrs. Boyd send a note to Joe specifying the amount of money that she had received; the young woman wanted to be certain that everyone knew she did, indeed, give all of each check to the Boyds. She visited the Boyds for several years until one day, Mrs. Boyd accused her of stealing a small amount of money from a bureau. The young woman was deeply hurt and, through tears, told Mr. Boyd that she thought it best not to continue her visits.

People in Joe's local office also became interested in the Boyds. His boss became acquainted with them, and in emergencies they frequently went to him. When their house was robbed in 1971 and their wedding bands stolen, Mrs. Boyd visited his office to request a loan, for she wanted to replace the rings quickly; instead, the man payed for the new rings himself.

A secretary in the office, Mrs. Wouters, became their steadfast friend. At first, she visited only intermittently, bringing groceries and, sometimes, money. As her children grew up and left home, she began to visit regularly, reading their mail to them, taking them to the bank once a month to cash their checks, acting as liaison with various companies when the Boyds have a problem, and discussing with Mrs. Boyd the situations that upset her. Mrs. Wouters says she loves the Boyds very much and enjoys the time she spends with them. She also says that she has "weathered many crises" with them, for during the 10 years she has known them, their lives have rarely been so smooth as they are now, and Mrs. Boyd has rarely been so calm and untroubled.

Mrs. Boyd's present contentedness, and the financial security that Mrs. Wouters feels is at its core, did not begin so auspiciously. In August 1977, Mrs. Boyd received a letter from a lawyer in Tennessee and a copy of her mother's will. A hard of hearing, partially-sighted friend who lives next door could not read the small print, so Mrs. Boyd presented the letter to Mrs. Wouters, who quickly recognized that something was amiss. The old will stipulated that all of her mother's property and assets were to be placed in a trust fund for her three unmarried daughters who, she felt, because of their disabilities, were less able than her other children to provide for themselves. If any of the women died, her portion would be used to increase the allowance to the surviving daughters or given to any dependent children. After the death of the third sister, the remainder of the estate would be divided among the mother's descendants, in accordance with the inheritance laws of the State of Tennessee. Mrs. Boyd's late brother Ralph was designated as original trustee.

Mrs. Wouters realized that a legal tangle was about to begin. She had known the Boyds long enough to be certain that Mrs. Boyd was unaware of any bequeathal. In 1973, Mrs. Boyd's only surviving sister, Helen, who still lived with her family in Tennessee, informed Mrs. Boyd that their brother Chester (the only brother still living, and the second trustee after Ralphs' death) had sold one of the family farms. Mrs. Boyd wrote to him, demanding some money from the sale. Chester told her that the sum was small and gave her only a few hundred dollars in token payment.

Mrs. Wouters brought the will to her own lawyer, who made contact with an attorney in Tennessee, "my high class lawyer," as Mrs. Boyd refers to him. After Chester's death in 1976, a niece's husband had been named executor of the estate. It seems that the nephew's lawyer had forwarded the will to Mrs. Boyd, requesting that she sign a document relinquishing her rights to her inheritance. With Mrs. Wouters' intervention and patient explanations of legal terminology, Mrs. Boyd has been made fully aware of the situation. Twice during 1977 and 1978, she flew to Tennessee to participate in court proceedings. Shortly afterward, she began receiving monthly checks of $1,000 as interim payments until the court decides how to interpret the will and safeguard Mrs. Boyd's rights. (Her family had not tampered with their mother's money; they seem to have been holding it until all of the sisters named in the will have died.)

Mrs. Wouters and others who know Mrs. Boyd say that she became impassioned when she first learned of the 35 year deception. Although she still feels angry and hurt about having been "cheated," her feelings are now contained. As when she discusses her former poverty, it seems that she has, in retrospect, lost or forgotten the intensity of her problems and perturbation; that she tends to regard many of the rather extraordinary particulars of her life with some detachment; or that she is simply oblivious to the uniqueness of those circumstances.

Because of that seeming distance from the past events of her own life, it is difficult to judge how much the Boyds have needed the help they have received. Mrs. Boyd is quite casual about it. Asked what they would have done without Joe's assistance, she replies, "We would have been very poor." If she did not have Mrs. Wouters with her now, she says, "I would ask the bank guard and a witness to help us at the bank. I would have to call the Housing Board (managers of the housing project) to read our mail to us." Her second statement probably reflects an unrealistic point of view. In addition, her own observations about the help she has received do not agree with Mrs. Wouters' assessment of the emotional support she has required over the years. There are rumblings from the deaf community that the Boyds can be very demanding in their requests for assistance. Mrs. Boyd does seem unaware of just how much of other people's voluntary time she uses. For example, the grocery store manager to whom they hand their shopping list spends as much as 4 hours gathering their groceries each week.

Mrs. Wouters feels that the sad part of Mrs. Boyd's newfound financial stability is that she has alienated her family. Throughout her 17 years in Florida, she had maintained pleasant, long-distance relationships with her sisters-in-law, nieces, and nephews, exchanging letters and gifts. When she found out about the will, she assumed that all of her many relatives knew what had happened, and she wrote them very bitter, accusatory letters. For awhile, all correspondence stopped, although her family has begun to write again. Mrs. Boyd still feels rather cold toward them, but says only, "Since the will, Mrs. Wouters does not enjoy reading their letters."

Alienating people by accusations is not a new problem for Mrs. Boyd. Although a certain amount of suspiciousness would seem natural after learning that members of one's family have been deceitful, all the while exhibiting a friendly attitude, people in her city say that Mrs. Boyd has always been suspicious of others; some go so far as to call it her "paranoia."

Long before the episode with the will, she was quick to accuse people of stealing things that a more objective observer might conclude were simply misplaced. Three years ago, she and her husband attended a camp-convention in Pittsburgh, Pennsylvania, sponsored by the National Association of the Deaf-Blind of America. She maintains that her bar of soap was stolen by the hearing-sighted interpreter-guides, some of whom not only volunteer their services for the several days of the convention, but also pay their own transportation and expenses. She feels so strongly about her soap having been stolen that she has refused to attend two subsequent conventions, although she and Mr. Boyd are now considering going to the next one, provided they can find a motel, rather than stay at the camp-convention site itself where she is sure other thefts will occur.

She is more vehement about the "cruel treatment" that she suffers in her own city. When Joe Chicca established the Boyds in their current home, he had a special telephone installed for them. The phone has no receiver, but the couple can dial different numbers to summon the city's fire and police departments, the manager of their housing project, or a local cab company. The calls all go through Security Systems, a private protection agency in their city. Despite long and patient discussions with Mrs. Wouters, Mrs. Boyd is firmly convinced that Security Systems pays people to cause trouble for her and her husband.

"I blame Security Systems. They give cruel treatment to the two of us. They pay a man at the grocery store to shove us in the legs with a grocery cart. It caused trouble with my veins. And cruel treatment on the bus. They shove us and push us. They want to make us fall. I told the police if we both fall and break our legs and hips, we'll sue Security Systems. It is their devilish behavior. They tell other people to bother us, push us. God and Jesus Christ are my Witness. They know their doings. I will let Them judge Security Systems. They will be sorry."

For many years she and her husband attended services at a church for the deaf. A deaf man picked them up, brought them to church and interpreted for them, but they had some trouble climbing the narrow steps into the building. "I stopped in 1976 because I almost fell. Mr. Jackson (the deaf man) tried and tried to make us fall down the high steps." She attributes his alleged misbehavior also to Security Systems. She is not altogether clear about why the protection agency wants to harm her. She vaguely mentions something having to do with Joe's having tempted the company with "money passed under the table" to provide extra services for the Boyds when they moved into their home. She also says, in what seems to be a more recent conclusion, that perhaps Joe pays Security Systems to hire people to push and shove her, because he believes that for the many years that he was giving them money, she and Mr. Boyd were aware she had an inheritance from her mother.

About a year ago, just before all of her trouble with the will, she and Mr. Boyd marched downtown to the mayor's office and presented him with a letter accusing Security

Systems of cruel treatment and demanding that city officials tell the security agency to stop the harassment. The mayor did talk with the director of the company, and some security officers went to the Boyd's home to check that everything was all right. Since then, Mrs. Boyd has had no trouble; she feels satisfied that the mayor's intervention has settled her difficulties.

Apart from Mrs. Boyd's tendency to be suspicious, and the help she receives from people like Joe and Mrs. Wouters, she and her husband seem to lead a normal life for an older couple, with certain adjustments. Mr. Boyd is 77 years old now and has become forgetful. Mrs. Boyd keeps him informed of everything that happens in their lives, and very patiently explains what she means again and again until he understands. His fingers have become less sensitive, so often she interprets their Braille reading into fingerspelling for him. He leaves the house alone to pick up what they need at the grocery store when they forget an item during their regular Saturday shopping. She, however, will not go out alone; she says, "I am afraid of bad men and thieves." Her reluctance sometimes seems like wifely devotion, for she says with full confidence that when Mr. Boyd dies, she will stay in Florida and do her shopping independently.

She has a regular schedule for doing the housework. "On Sunday I don't do any cleaning; we read Braille religious lessons. On Monday I cook and wash silk clothing in the sink, by hand. On Tuesday night I wash the white clothes in the washing machine. I put them in the dryer and go to bed. On Wednesday morning I take them from the dryer and put them away. Then I do the colored clothes. Wednesday afternoon, I iron shirts if they need it, the ones that are not permanent press. I used to hang them up outside, but they sometimes got caught in the rain. I didn't know when it started to rain. So now I always use the dryer. On Thursday, I clean the refrigerator. On Saturday we go to town, every Saturday on the bus. We buy shoes or clothes or whatever else we need. We eat at the lunch counter at Clairmont Department Store. I bring our food list to the grocery store and the manager gets our groceries. I pay by check. Then he calls us a cab and we go home."

Mrs. Boyd can distinguish most of her grocery items by the size and shape of the packaging. She has a special method for identifying her large cans of different-flavored juices. She shakes each can vigorously, then holds it very still; heavier juices settle more slowly than thinner ones. For the few that she cannot tell apart–apple juice and fruit punch–the manager tears off a piece of the label in a prearranged pattern.

"Once a month on Monday, Mrs. Wouters takes us to the bank. We cash our checks and put some money in our checking account. I take the rest in cash, $10 bills and $1 bills. I put them in different pockets of my billfold. When we want to see Mrs. Wouters for something else, or when my husband wants to see his sister, I send them a letter and tell them when to come." The Boyds then prop a cane by the door, the handle touching it, and the tip end near one of their hands at their reading chair. Energetic knocking produces vibrations, alerting the Boyds that their guests have arrived. Since a robbery when they were seated on their front porch, they keep their doors locked and their windows barred.

Reading is the Boyds' hobby. They subscribe to *The Voice*, the magazine published by the National Association of the Deaf-Blind of America; Mrs. Boyd enjoys keeping abreast of the activities of other deaf-blind people. They also receive a number of religious periodicals from various Protestant denominations; a news magazine from the Matilda Ziegler Foundation for the Blind in New York; and the sporadic *New York Times Braille Edition*, a synopsis of major international and national news. Mrs. Boyd is interested in political affairs and better informed than many well-educated people with far greater access to sources of information.

She and Mr. Boyd have traveled some. Twice in the late 1960's, they went to New York City by bus. They visited the Industrial Home for the Blind's workshop for deaf-blind clients, the American Foundation for the Blind, and the Matilda Ziegler Foundation offices. They also stopped once at Hackensack, New Jersey to visit a friend of Mrs. Boyd's family. They particularly enjoyed a tour of an Amish community in Pennsylvania, part of the National Association of the Deaf-Blind of America's convention that they attended. Mrs. Wouters has taken them to a nearby beach town but, in general, Mrs. Boyd is not anxious to leave her home and go to strange places. "I can't see or hear," she reminds her questioner.

    I had met the Boyds by chance in their grocery store the day before we were scheduled to begin the interviews. As they were waiting for the manager to return with their groceries, I introduced myself and we chatted. Then and later, too, Mrs. Boyd asked how I had known it was she and her husband in the store. I replied with what seemed an obvious explanation: they were signing into each other's hands, an indication that each was both deaf and blind. I assumed that there was not another deaf-blind couple of the same approximate ages in their town. Mrs. Boyd found it interesting that I had been able to identify them so easily. I learned later that she and Mr. Boyd had both assumed for several days that I was deaf, a not unlikely possibility since I sign and fingerspell. But Mr. Boyd also asked if I were blind. Their assumptions struck me as interesting, not because they have lost touch with reality, for that is certainly not the case. Their questions simply suggested that both of them have lived with deaf-blindness for so much of their lives, and have been able to avoid many of the pitfalls of isolation and loneliness, that to them, deaf-blindness is just another basic characteristic, not very much different from race or sex or age.

Wilbur Martinson*

Willie Martinson talks a lot about "Science." He explains that he is the "male block lead" in "Experimental Science," also known as "Science Empire Work," the "Science Empire Universe," "International Science and the Alliances," and, most commonly, "Advanced Science." He has been a "High Frequency Science Student" since he was spotted, as an 8-year-old in 1922, by military officers when his aunt's car broke down near an Army installation at Fort Burns, Iowa. The government began work on his "atoms, tissues, raw flesh, and membranes" in 1932, causing him to become "diseased in science" and to lose his vision and hearing. He did not, however, become aware of his role in "Radar Mind Research" until the end of 1945.

Throughout his long–and not entirely voluntary–career, Willie has been known by code names such as "Uncle Sam," "Red Jack," and "Brown Wolf." For several years he signed letters, "W. J. Martinson and Colleague, Radar Science Executives of Radar Researches of the World." That "Colleague," the "female block lead" with whom he can communicate only through brain waves, currently uses the code name "Roberta." Together they were instrumental in the development of five "Mind Machines"–"Radar," "Sonar," "Exaver," "Tomorrow," and "Whatnot"–which collectively provide the United States Government with surveillance

*Names of people and places have been changed, including cities, towns, states, state agencies, and the state hospital.

and testing possibilities in every layer of land, sea, and atmosphere.

Willie explains that the experimentation network to which he belongs embraces some five million other individuals, most of whom, like him, were made deaf-blind by "Compulsory Science"; several thousand of the other "Science Students" are otherwise disabled or in prisons. With them, Willie has served the country from the end of World War I, through World War II, and the Korean and Vietnam conflicts. He is currently involved with the confrontation in the Middle East and has, in fact, "blown and shot down the Arabs two times here in Amos, Iowa." Although he is usually the passive subject of radar experimentation, he intends to "give the Palestinians part of Egypt," and to "put lots of homeless Black Africans back on the old ground of their lost land." Another of his projects is the study of the pace of living, called "Forward March."

Willie is 64 years old, profoundly deaf and nearly totally blind. (He can perceive hand movement in the periphery of his right eye at a distance no greater than 5 inches.) He lives at Reicher's Rest Home, a 100-year-old farmhouse 20 miles from Des Moines, Iowa. He has been there 14 years, paying room and board from his earnings as a brushmaker with the Iowa Services for the Blind.

Prior to his move to the home in 1964, Willie spent 19 years–19 years and 6 weeks, as he says–in the Des Moines State Hospital. He was initially hospitalized for delusions and aberrant, potentially dangerous behavior. Although the delusions have persisted for more than 30 years, it was not long after his committal that the hospital's psychiatric staff determined he was basically sane and capable of living outside the institution. More than 10 years passed, however, from their first attempts to place him in a boarding house until the time he actually left the hospital.

In the meantime, Willie worked both in the hospital and at the Services for the Blind workshop. He opened a bank account, shopped in local stores, and ordered equipment through the mail. He set up a carpentry shop in the hospital's basement, tapping their electric system. He sent his clothes out for better laundry service than the hospital provided. He consulted a lawyer about paying taxes on his income and, through his own initiative, paid room and board at the institution.

Willie's voice is raspy and difficult for those who do not know him well to understand. (For that reason, he responded to most of the questions I printed in his palm by typing, a system he devised after I told him I could not understand his voice.) When he talks (and types) his responses are generally brief and to the point. At the same time, he expresses himself in a rather grandiose manner, particularly when referring to characters and events of his delusion. He also peppers his remarks with liberal doses of "goddamned," "son of a gun," and "numbskull." While this directness and his voice make him seem gruff, he is a patient and kind man.

Willie was born May 15, 1914 in Lorraine, Iowa. (He is very precise about dates and money, always giving full information in months and days, dollars and cents, even for events and business transactions that occurred 20 or 40 years ago.) His parents were farmers of Dutch, German, English, and Irish stock. He spent his early years on farms they owned; later, with the Depression, he worked on land they rented. He attended grade school at a consolidated district schoolhouse and had 2 years of high school, during which he maintained an "A" average.

The etiologies of his sensory losses are uncertain, although the deafness has been attributed to radical mastoidectomies. During his institutionalization at the state hospital, one neurologist hypothesized that the dual loss resulted from the Arnold-Chiari Syndrome, a malformation of the brain and spinal cord that frequently causes minor visual problems.

Willie's first indication of the vision impairment occurred at the beginning of high school. Objects seemed to "shimmer" before his eyes. At about the same time, he relates, "Had ears and tonsils pussy. Had tonsils removed in 1929 summer (he was 15) and went back to school to try examinations. Ears, in end of freshman year, draining, and was sent on train to Gambrill, Iowa, to look for ear aid. Could just notice some ear deafness. I doctored at Gambrill 'till June 26, 1931, and Dad took me to the Research Institute in Des Moines. I had x-ray photos and showed major mastoids on both sides. Was operated on and in hospital 10 days. Was turned out to go home. I helped some with harvest and soon took tractor to plow for neighbor half section of wheat land. Started to school in fall of 1931, was hard of hearing and could not hear conversations in rooms. Tried it my way and failed out at semester examination." He continues, "Just then, January 15, 1932, they ("Advanced Science") cast on to me a seizure of eyes and hearing and left me deaf and three-quarters blind on the left side; could see most fairly well on right side of right eye."

Willie's mother had died in 1928, and in 1930 his father married Mary Hannah Waterstone, a schoolteacher whom Willie calls a "numbskull." He had an older sister (now a nurse in Iowa City); his father and stepmother had two sons during the 1930's. It is impossible to reconstruct exactly what happened in Willie's relationship with his family–to know if his present resentment accurately reflects events of 40 years ago or even his perceptions, at that time, of how he was treated. It seems likely that the chaos of those years–with the Depression, his father's remarriage, the reduction in communication caused by his disabilities, and the emotional upheaval he must have experienced all occurring more or less simultaneously–added a certain distortion to his interpretation of events.

Willie believes that he was cheated out of his inheritance from his natural mother's estate; he accuses his father of stealing the money to renovate a house and barn for his new wife. Willie says, "The father Johnny Robert was mean and one-sided and stingy. He hinted he wanted $1,200 out of me for doctors' bills. Had not been that much, but I turned him 12 females and 2 steer calves in April 1932. He said, 'Hell, it was not half enough.' I did not ask relatives (his father and stepmother) for wages or such as interests of estate. Wasn't given any since was livestock and small patches of farming." Willie also complained about his stepmother's management of the house. "I was told to keep quiet about the way it looked. I did not crab or fight the family, but they did not favor me."

After he became disabled and quit school, Willie worked on his father's farm. "Worked at chores–fences, feeding, hauling manure, husking corn, etc. Could not see well enough to cultivate small plants." During the late 1930's, however, he began to send letters to various state and county agencies, seeking aid in finding work. According to later records at the state hospital, the tone of the letters revealed an urgent need to become independent from his father.

In 1938, Willie was given a job as a "U" class laborer through the National Youth Recovery Act, digging irrigation ditches, mixing grasshopper poison, clearing a cemetery, and cleaning sewage. He says, "Could still see well enough to get along with autos on country roads and work with team." When he was 26, presumably through letters he had written, he came to the attention of the state agency for the blind. During that summer, 1940, he attended a 10-week session of the state school for the blind where he learned Braille. A note in his hospital file states that while at the school he "didn't accept his limitations." The following year, George Carlson, director of the state agency, found him a job making egg crates for a packing company. Until the business folded shortly afterward, Willie worked, boarding in a nearby town and riding a horse to the farm where the company was located. He was suspicious and resentful for he was paid lower wages than the other laborers, but George Carlson remembers that, because of his poor vision, Willie's work was inferior.

After another stint on his father's farm Willie bought himself a "shoesmith" (a portable piece of equipment holding all tools necessary for repairing shoes) and established a business repairing shoes in Gambrill, Iowa. His shop was in a building on Main Street. He painted his shop and the building's stairwells in exchange for rent, and boarded in a house six blocks away. His landlady later recalled that he had been moody and depressed; he was particularly disheartened at having no girl friend and being unable to serve in the Armed Forces during World War II. After 3 months, Willie found that he could not afford to keep the shop, and again he returned to his father's farm.

With his dogged independence and deepening feelings of inadequacy, this last return must have been extremely trying. Though he rarely talks about his feelings, he does say, "After losing my hearing and vision I was most downhearted and denied in each case. The families and friends began to doubt and neglect. Was no earnings and no employments of which were ambitions. The whole life seemed to be in a stump." He continued to write letters, but this time seeking not only employment but also assistance in joining the Seabees. He found it difficult to tolerate his half brothers, 9 and 12 years old. He considered them irresponsible, especially with his property, and argued with them frequently. About his stepmother and the boys, he says, "Were city quitting folks and unwilling to toil. Darrell once hit me with an air rifle and she let him out of it. The whole outfits blamed all messes on me. The stepmother and father got awful tired of me, and stepbrothers kept quarrelling and blaming it on me. They were close, and scolded a lot of money. They did not raise much and I knew who it belonged to, and did not ask foolish questions and kept out of trouble, but they never came back to settle with me regardless."

In 1945, Willie was sent to the state mental hospital. He attributes his committal there to his family's greed, and to a lesser degree, their intentional obstruction of his "Advanced Science" work. He says, "It appears the relatives stalled me in asylum to hold me and take my property and savings. I had only some less than $1,299 at that time, but it was mine and I could use it. I did not have to keep the "shoesmith" but I wanted it that way. I was working on the farm. Kids (the half brothers) were dragging into my junk. After so long, they ("Advanced Science") told me to kick out a north window. A short time later, law officials came and hauled me away and never gave me any court hearing. I paid $5 for window in a few minutes without troubles, but they got the law. All that trouble of which went with window was no licks struck." Willie says that he was held from May 13 until May 16, 1945, in the county jail, then "hauled" to the "insane asylum."

Another version of Willie's committal to the state hospital is supplied by the hospital medical records, and is corroborated in part by Willie's enduring delusion about "Mental Science." According to the information his father provided the hospital, Willie had become "peculiar" about 2 months before his committal. He would set out to do something, then seem to forget what he had intended.

On April 23, 1945, he left his bed at 10:30 (the records do not stipulate morning or evening) and walked 29 miles. When his father found him, Willie said that he did not know where he was or where he was going. His father brought him home and put him to bed. Willie was in a coma for 2 weeks. When he came to, he said the Nazis were after him with a "radio mind machine" and he was going to be killed by the Germans. His parents caught him trying to climb out of an upstairs bedroom window. He said that he had a military secret he had to relay to the Army officers at Fort Burns. When his parents refused to call the installation, he threatened his father as, the report notes, he continued to do several more times after "losing his mind." He then told his family to forget what he had said and never to mention it again. He began talking to himself, reviewing his life.

There are later notes in the hospital file that he also climbed on top of a windmill and threatened to jump, and that he hiked several miles in the snow. His family thought he might have developed a tumor or blood clot on the brain. With his strange behavior and, what to them was his new bitterness toward his father, they thought he might be dangerous and sent him to the state hospital on May 13, 1945. There is no record of a confinement in jail.

During his first weeks at the hospital, Willie continued to talk irrationally about the war, Germans, and his childhood. According to records, he said that his mind had been equipped with "compression apparatus–a concealed TV" and that he had to walk to Chicago, presumably to deliver top secret information. Early interviews determined that he had a good command of "school knowledge"; that he could supply accurate biographical information; and that he was "not unduly excited, euphoric, depressed, or indifferent." The possibility of a brain tumor was acknowledged; the examining psychiatrist also noted that an operation had caused "organic changes leading to deaf-blindness," but the surgery was "too remote to have caused the psychotic episode." (By this time, Willie's vision had deteriorated to acuity of 20/200, limited to his right periphery. To read the psychiatrist's written questions, he wore a jeweler's magnifying glass and held papers a microinch from it.) The suggested diagnosis was "Psychosis due to unknown (or hereditary) causes, but associated with organic changes." The psychiatrist further noted that Willie's "attacks of the delusion were general in onset, increasing, and variable with rational intervals."

If the variability of Willie's behavior was not remarkable for an inmate of a state hospital, certainly many of his daily activities were. Within weeks of his arrival, he assumed the responsibility of making beds on his ward. Shortly afterward, he was polishing floors with an electric buffer, carrying laundry sacks, and washing dishes in the kitchen. He became friends with Bess Sherman, the hospital's dietician. As time went on, she found him to be a "meticulous and effective" worker and gave him steady assignments scrubbing floors; filling flour bins; cleaning tables, chairs, and countertops; hauling canned foods on a wagon; and carting out the garbage. Before long he was working 10 hours a day.

During the nineteen forties and early fifties, Willie continued to talk about "Advanced Science." In an early letter home he told his family that he was living with Anna, the wife whom God had given him. He told them, too, that in 1945 he had had a vision of the beautiful girl who operated his "mind machine"; he realized then that for years he had unknowingly been part of "Advanced Science's" mind experimentation. He also wrote letters to state and federal authorities–the hospital's superintendent and attorney, the "State Board of Mental Examiners," and the U.S. Justice Department in Washington, D.C.–informing them that he, the "Chief Executive of Radar Science Research," was incarcerated against his will and demanding to be released.

From the records, there seems to have been minimal contact between Willie and the hospital's psychiatrists–certainly little that was therapeutic. One doctor noted that Willie became "hostile" when it was suggested that he stop writing his letters. For some time he had been "combative" when his clothes disappeared from his room, but as the hospital instituted better security, he calmed down. Another psychiatrist, who wrote about him for several years, noted that occasionally Willie would respond to his attempts at conversation with "spontaneously produced paranoid ideas," asking, "Do you know about the 'Institute for Brain Waves' and have you ever heard about the 'Allied Statistical Defense System' of which I am commander?" He rejected all attempts to discuss his family, and was reported to be antagonistic toward the psychiatrists or to avoid them altogether.

In 1950, a supervising psychiatrist informed the ward psychiatrist that he did not want Willie's delusional system attacked. He wrote,

"This really capable person has erected this defense against an overpoweringly discouraging tragedy to his life, and can meet with it the real loss of productivity that his deformity has made."

Although his choice of words may not be acceptable to disabled individuals today, his instructions mark the transition point in how Willie was regarded and treated by the hospital's staff. His ward psychiatrist began to compliment him on his work in the kitchen; this doctor told Willie he would no longer ask personal questions, and that he would be of service in whatever way possible. Willie began to approach the doctor to chat and to request small favors. In a curious note several months later, a social worker stated that "the patient's behavior has improved because of help from his doctor in adjusting to his handicap."

Not long afterward, George Carlson, director of the state agency for the blind, invited the hospital to send vision-impaired inmates to his workshop for part-time employment. The workshop was located about a half mile from the hospital on the same state property. Thus Willie began the work making rubber mats and brushes that he has continued for 25 years. With this temporary employment that he managed to extend indefinitely, he began to divide his time between the hospital kitchen and the workshop. During the nineteen fifties, the new general manager of the Services for the Blind workshop, Bob Lawrence, became acquainted with Willie and gave him space to work on his own carpentry projects. Willie designed various items, including birdhouses and leather-covered stools that he gave to his friends in the hospital kitchen and at Services for the Blind. Bob says that Willie always insisted on paying for the scrap material he used, and that he had a good sense of how much things were worth.

In the meantime, Willie learned from correspondence with his family that they were not paying their share of his hospital bill. At that time, the hospital required patients' relatives to pay a certain percentage of the bill to cover living expenses. Willie was concerned, and talked with someone who told him that his work in the kitchen would be accepted in partial payment of the debt, that, by the mid-fifties, had accumulated to over $1,000. The person may have been humoring Willie; he took the answer seriously. He also began to make payments to the hospital's bookkeeping office from his piecework earnings at Services for the Blind. A psychiatrist, learning of the payments, called the workshop to inquire about Willie's earnings. For 2 months' labor he had received $100, of which he paid the hospital $50. When the doctor asked Willie what he had done with the other $50, Willie became incensed. He answered, though, that he had put it in his bank account. (Willie says now, about his relatives and his institutionalization, "Their idea cost me $15,016.72, of which I paid $7,870 cash and traded institution work for remainder." The hospital's business records do show some $7,000 written off in 1972 as uncollectable. Although what remains of earlier monthly payment records does not indicate who made the payments, there is no reason to doubt that, with the exception of a few hundred dollars his father sent, Willie contributed the rest of the money himself.

As early as 1953, the various psychiatrists who handled Willie's case had noted that he *could* be released if an appropriate living situation were found for him—a rest home or boarding house where he would be looked after. They stipulated, however, that his residence would have to be located within walking distance of the Services for the Blind workshop and on the same side of any busy streets, to lessen the possibility of Willie's injuring himself on his way to work. Allusions to his leaving the hospital appear in each year's records through the fifties. Interspersed with those notes, however, are pronouncements from each new psychiatrist Willie meets that the "patient" is "insane" and the likelihood of his leaving the hospital successfully is slim.

Judgments about Willie's sanity, delivered after very brief contact with him, range from an early *"dementia praecox,* catatonic probably," through "he has made a brittle adjustment and shows tremendous hostility," to "judgment and insight impaired." One psychiatrist, learning that Willie had ordered a tricycle from New York, which he used to ride on the state grounds between the hospital and Services for the Blind, wrote that the "patient" is pleased with his "new toy." A regular pattern appears in the records, though; all the doctors who stayed on the ward long enough to know Willie and learn about his independent life eventually concurred that he really *could* leave the hospital. By the mid-fifties, the social work staff had started to look for a boarding house, but finding none available in the specified proximity to the Services for the Blind workshop, they abandoned the search for several years.

In March of 1958, Willie bought himself a "shopsmith" (a compact piece of equipment including a table saw, lathe, drill press, and other items necessary for carpentry work) for, he recounts, "$303.64, plus $1 delivery fee." He had it delivered to the Services for the Blind workshop, then asked one of the truck drivers there to bring it to the hospital for him. Bob Lawrence's employees knew there was an "understanding" about Willie—he could have what he wanted. Willie had them leave it in the hospital's basement, in a tunnel near the kitchen. There he hooked it up with the hospital's power system. He had other equipment downstairs that he had been acquiring and using for several years—a table and stool; hand tools (he used a short-handled hammer for he could not see well enough to control the longer kind); a miter box and saw; extension cords and clamps; a large movie theater-type popcorn machine that he had bought secondhand some years before; and skeleton keys and picklocks that opened the hospital's tin shop, electric shop, electric supply cupboards, and various other storerooms and cabinets.

For more than 6 months, Willie used the shop in his spare time, building things for his friends. At one point he created pandemonium in the kitchen when he tried to install a mechanized conveyor belt to move garbage through the room quickly. All this time he held his two jobs. One psychiatrist noted that Willie was "rather obscure"—one had to leave notes for him because he was always off working somewhere. In November 1958, however, the carpentry shop was discovered. Amid uproar and censure, Willie's equipment was put into storage with the understanding that it would be returned to him when he left the hospital. Willie was both enraged and dejected. Throughout the fifties, he had continued to talk about "Advanced Science," elaborating, it seems, on his earlier conceptions. He wrote his angry letters, however, only when something was bothering him.

Now he started to send them again, demanding to be released from the hospital. (These were to government agencies; he seems to have stopped writing to his family some years before.)

Again the social work office was asked to find Willie a place to live. This time, one observant psychiatrist realized that, since Willie had been finding his way around town for years—going to the bank, shopping, employing a lawyer to advise him about his income tax—perhaps it would not be necessary for him to live so near the Services for the Blind workshop. Although Willie now says, "The mental institution can become a home and it can be lived," his own efforts to leave went beyond his letters. In 1951 he had "escaped." When hospital authorities recovered him some 20 miles away, he said that he had been going home to find work. By the late fifties, in addition to the social workers, his friend from the kitchen, Bess Sherman, was searching for a place for him. She told him about an Air Force base that was selling used trailers. Willie wrote asking if he should not have priority in getting one since he was "President of Radar Researches of America." His pyschiatrist during this period suspected that he was also investigating neighborhoods around the hospital to find an appropriate home.

In 1959, the social workers found a place and it seemed that Willie would soon be moving. The owner of a nearby rest home was willing to accept Willie; in addition, her son owned a stone veneer production business where Willie might be employed. Willie was informed of the opportunity to move and, after a few days' consideration, told hospital officials that he did want to go to the rest home. A psychiatrist's note provides a jarring reminder of the power other people had over aspects of Willie's life, and their attitudes toward his perception of his independence. With some amusement, the doctor wrote that Willie said he had "decided" that, yes, he would move to Mrs. Grishom's.

A lawyer in town agreed to become Willie's guardian—for some reason his father could not remain in that role. Just as it seemed that everything was settled, the lawyer discovered that the judge handling the transfer of guardianship had taken some shortcuts and the papers were not valid. During the months it took to rectify the errors, the owner of the rest home changed her mind. The hospital staff concluded that, with his delusion, Willie did need to remain in the hospital after all.

For several years things continued more or less as they had been. Willie had no shop, but he worked at his two jobs. The records become less complete at this point, but no doubt Willie wrote frequently about "Advanced Science" and complaining about his "incarceration." One way or another, however, he let Bob Lawrence, manager of the Services for the Blind workshop, know that he was still upset at having lost the shop. Bob is the business director of the workshop, not a counselor; for a long time, though, he had taken a personal interest in Willie. He went to the hospital to see what could be worked out. To his surprise, he learned that Willie was free to leave, if a living situation could be found for him.

Bob spent about one year investigating various possibilities, but could find no rest home or boarding house that would accept a deaf-blind, somewhat "eccentric" 50-year-old man who must have access to his power tools. Finally, he remembered Mrs. Reicher and her rest home. Bob had grown up in the country not far from her ranch. He knew she ran a rest home for a variety of people who, when it comes down to it, have no place else to go. Bob remembers that when he approached Margaret Reicher and described Willie to her, "She didn't bat an eye. She said, 'Bring him over.'"

Since 1954, Mrs. Reicher has run the rest home on her 2,400 acre ranch. For years before that, she and her husband, who died in 1967, had bought up farming acreage and pasture land adjacent to their original property. The farms included the previous owners' homes. In the fifties, an out-of-town couple rented one large farmhouse to start a small, 10 to 20 bed nursing home. When the Reichers discovered the tenants' scandalous negligence and mismanagement, they asked them to leave and themselves assumed operation of the home. Throughout the years, the rest home residents have been old people–many of them senile or nonambulatory–and inmates from the state hospital who authorities felt could not benefit from psychiatric care but who needed some supervision and, as Mrs. Reicher puts it, "tender loving care."

She and her husband welcomed Willie from the start. Within months of his arrival, Mr. Reicher, with financial assistance from the state agency for the blind, converted an old bunkhouse just behind the main house into Willie's workshop. Bob Lawrence was thinking of their renovating the building for Willie when he approached Mrs. Reicher. The state agency brought over the machinery Willie needed to make rubber mats; it is on indefinite loan to him. They also delivered his personal equipment that had been in storage at the hospital—including his popcorn machine. He later got his old "shoesmith."

Work remains Willie's foremost activity and his greatest pleasure. When he gets a delivery of new materials to assemble into brushes (he has not made rubber mats for some time), he may work 14 hours a day until the supplies are exhausted. He has made birdhouses, rabbit hutches, and elaborate aluminum and wooden doghouses for the yard. He bought an old car from a woman who works at the rest home and, without assistance, removed the engine. Mrs. Reicher once bought him some scrap lumber and, that same day, he built plant boxes for her greenhouse. On another occasion, he took apart an old freezer and with its various parts made toys for the cook's daughter. Once he designed a wooden door for the home's storm and fruit cellar, using laths for measuring; he built the framed structure, attached scrap iron handles that he bent by hand, painted it, and hung it himself. His craftsmanship is remarkable, particularly since his vision declined again in the early sixties and he can perceive only shapes and motion within inches from his eye. (He says, "On January 15, 1962, they again cut onto sight of right eye. It has weakened and I cannot read paper with my glass.")

Willie refuses to accept welfare money. When he left the state hospital in 1964, the county made four payments to him, totaling $292.25. He sent the checks back, but they were returned and finally, grudgingly, he agreed to accept them. He does take Social Security disability benefits that he earned during his previous employment—$169.40 a month. He earns about $200 more through Services for the Blind. He pays the rest home $245 for room, board, laundry, and housekeeping. An additional expense is $14.65 each month for the anti-depressant pills he has been taking since the late fifties. Until recently he did receive Medicaid to cover his medicine, but since he has accumulated $3,000 in his savings account ("$3,002.13"), that aid has been curtailed. Mrs. Reicher charges him $50 a month less than the other residents, all but one of whom are on county assistance, because his livelihood is marginal; she lets him earn the difference from the chores-like garbage-burning and carpentry projects-that he relishes. (She watches from a window when he burns the garbage on a windy day.)

Willie has his quirks. He is perhaps unduly suspicious of other residents of the home and keeps a lock on his workshop door for which even Mrs. Reicher has no key. She, wisely it seems, has always had a witness present when conducting financial transactions with him. When he gets mail, he always has it transliterated (printed into his palm) twice-perhaps by Mrs. Reicher one evening, then one of the housecleaners the following day. Printing a two-page letter into Willie's hand may require a good hour, but no one seems to begrudge him the time or inconveniences caused by either his deaf-blindness or his beliefs in "Advanced Science."

Mrs. Reicher's feeling for Willie is obvious-and understandable. Each Christmas, he gives a $1 bill to each of the home's other residents, although, except for one woman, Mary, he has no social relationships with them. Willie pays Mary to do some sewing for him, and Mrs. Reicher assumes it is through conversations with her that Willie learns the gossip of the rest home. (Mary writes a column about events at the home for the local newspaper. Until Mrs. Reicher gently suggested that she needed help with the newspaper work and with her garden, and invited the woman's aid, Mary had spent all of her time in bed with the covers drawn over her face.) When the 4-H Club comes to visit, Willie always gives them some of his brushes. The group sells the items for fundraising and has tried to give him some money, but he refuses it. Mrs. Reicher has told them to bring him raw materials to work with-those are what he really wants. In addition to Bob Lawrence who sees Willie regularly on business, Bess Sherman, who has retired from her position as dietician at the state hospital, sometimes visits. Once she brought small bagfuls of assorted fruits, giving him the opportunity to select different treats for a week. Willie insisted that the favors be included in a salad for all the residents to enjoy. When his father and stepmother or his sister bring him ice cream, he has it served to everyone at suppertime.

Mrs. Reicher's observations of Willie's family offer some support that his own perceptions of their mistreatment are biased. She says that his parents used to visit every 3 or 4 months until recently when they have both become ill. His sister stops by on her way to see the older couple, but Willie continues to feel, "She is not at odds with me, but she does not care much for me." When she sends him Christmas presents, he sends their monetary equivalent in return.

Willie does not talk much about his own feelings. When he has a toothache or something is bothering him—as when his roommate was keeping rabbits outside and Willie was convinced that lice were infesting his bedroom—he sits upstairs at his typewriter composing letters. Mrs. Reicher has learned to recover and read the papers he crumbles and throws away; amid details about "Advanced Science" she generally finds a clue to the more immediate problem.

When his feelings about spending 19 years at the state hospital or his current situation at the rest home are solicited, Willie betrays little emotion. Assumptions about what has been painful in his life must be made from the particulars of his delusion—that in "Advanced Science" he has a "Colleague," and that his "Colleague" is female; that with the other "Compulsory Science Students" he belongs to a community; that he serves his government, and thus other people, in a highly productive, important capacity and is, in fact, involved in the most important of world affairs; and, if it is not assuming too much, that there is an external entity responsible for his deaf-blindness and concomitant losses. About all Willie volunteers regarding his feelings is, "It has been a lonely life in the Sciences. Is this: no one close understands what all is about. The life of working in handicap for relatives and Compulsory Sciences and Researches is something of which will tie you down and of which seldom does anyone emerge."

Mrs. Reicher sometimes feels that the rest home is a bigger headache for her than it is worth. The residents now are all from the state hospital and many have spent only the required 90 days there before being sent to her. Without skills in group living, they often do not behave appropriately for a rest home environment. In addition, the fees she charges do not always meet the expenses of maintaining the house and paying the cook's and housecleaner's salaries. When she thinks of giving it up, though, as she did quite seriously when her husband died, something stops her. She asks, "Where else is there for Willie-and some of the others-to go? Where is another place he could have his workshop and be free to live as he wants?"

Conclusion

Drawing conclusions can be dangerous–but not drawing conclusions can be more dangerous. Many issues appear repeatedly in these profiles, to the point that patterns of experience and response begin to emerge in the lives of the people interviewed. That recurrence alone warrants the issues' further examination.

Isolation, dependence, anger, and resentment are present in the lives of most of those interviewed, but for no one are they so all consuming to completely control and define the person. The individuals have remained individuals, largely through the process of adjustment to their losses and limitations. A person's adjustment depends in part on experiences before becoming deaf-blind–personality, self-image, and feelings about disabilities in general or specifically deaf-blindness. Adjustment depends, too, on situations encountered as a deaf-blind person, including societal attitudes reflected in other people's behavior and the public policies that affect everyday experiences. The inevitable reduction in communication inherent in deaf-blindness has an inestimable impact on a person's life; input and exchange that are tremendously restricted can redirect an individual's experiences in unfathomable ways.

Isolation is an unavoidable reality in the lives of deaf-blind people. For most, the loneliness and alienation is massive and unrelieved. One theme emerging from the interviews is the relationship among rejection, withdrawal, and isolation. One way that people deal with rejection, obvious or subtle, is to avoid the contact that makes it possible. That reaction occurs among people who are aware of their disabilities and have learned to understand other people's attitudes and their own discomfort. It occurs even more frequently among those with Usher's Syndrome. Most people with Usher's Syndrome report teasing and rejection by other students when they were in school. Often, it seems, the young person with Usher's Syndrome, unaware of the vision impairment and, ironically, unable to *see* that his behavior is different from his peers', has nothing to attach the teasing to and thus, no explanation for why he is rejected. He withdraws. The longer any individual remains detached from a group, the more difficult it becomes for the group to include him, and the more painful it becomes for him to risk further rejection.

Another factor in the deaf-blind person's isolation is differentness. The person with Usher's Syndrome, who has grown up in schools for the deaf and shares a language with other deaf people, would ordinarily belong to the deaf community. Yet often he is regarded, and regards himself, as not only *different*, but *strange* or a *mistake*. When neither the deaf-blind person nor a community, however, considers him unique, he experiences less isolation. (In parts of Louisiana where estimations of the incidence of Usher's Syndrome in the deaf population reach as high as 30 percent [due to patterns of consanguinity during previous generations], deaf-blind people seem to accept their condition more easily and the deaf community seems to involve them more readily.)

Some loss of autonomy is another inevitable reality of deaf-blindness. As the deaf-blind person is forced to become increasingly solitary, his physical restrictions and societal structures and attitudes prevent him from becoming independent. The individual with extremely limited hearing and vision must depend on others for managing money, shopping for food, reading mail, relaying what the doctor says, informing him of changes in his bus route—daily activities that seem trivial until obstacles in their performance expose their significance. Frequently, only a few people in his community can communicate with the deaf-blind person and then, not always fluently. One or two people become exclusive helpers, creating a burden for them and breeding suspiciousness and resentment in the dependent person. It may be more remarkable that most deaf-blind people are not paranoid than it is that some are.

Bitterness is a phase many deaf-blind people recall passing through, and they explain it as envy of others combined with their own feelings of inadequacy. Some deaf-blind people remain resentful, and their anger is focused primarily at their families. It seems that at the core of the resentment is the deaf-blind person's feeling of having been abandoned by those who, our culture teaches, will always be accepting, helpful, and supportive, regardless of circumstance. Deaf-blind people frequently charge that their families do not communicate or will not: they do not learn the methods of communicating or they do not interpret what is happening around them. In some cases families are insensitive, but the burden imposed on them cannot be overlooked. Similarly, some deaf-blind people are obstinate in their opinions and demands for assistance. Perhaps because he does not receive sufficient feedback from others about their feelings, or adequate reminders that the world is a hectic place, the deaf-blind person loses an accurate perception of the validity of multiple points of view and of what are reasonable expectations of others. Yet if the deaf-blind person does not express needs and preferences forcefully, he will be overlooked and forgotten.

In adjusting to the deaf-blindness, many individuals interviewed seem to have experienced all or some of the stages of adjustment described in the rehabilitation literature: shock, disbelief, denial, anger, bargaining, mourning, and acceptance. Other methods of adjustment are also common. Religious faith has been the primary support of several people. Some expressed a feeling of security that God is protecting them; others feel that although they cannot understand why they are deaf-blind, they can accept their condition as God's order and thus find meaning in an otherwise incomprehensible situation. At the same time, many isolated people have found in a strong church community other people willing to communicate with them and accept them. Several people expressed hope that they will recover their hearing or vision. While such hope might be considered denial of the disabilities and refusal to accept their finality, its appearance among several people who explain it without delusion suggests that it is, too, an adaptive coping.

People have also lowered their expectation—learned to live from day to day. They learn to be content with living smoothly, and doing that alone may require a major effort each day. Considering the tremendous impact of deaf-blindness, the ability to lower expectation, far from being a passive resignation, implies a remarkable human resilience in responding to adversity. At the same time, without a single exception, the people interviewed expressed, most of them verbally, the desire to be productive and to have friends—to work and to love. As deaf-blindness and societal barriers reduce a person's options, those two basic needs become foremost.

Despite its importance, the deaf-blind individual's adjustment to the disability is only part of the story. He is confronted by outside obstacles daily. If the deaf-blind person is to do more than simply survive, his adjustment must be complemented with some accommodation by the world he lives in. The deaf-blind person's needs are many: accessible public transportation; inclusion, through interpreters or individualized programs, in educational and social activities; reliable means of shopping, handling finances, and performing other tasks of daily living—and assistance provided in a way that physical reliance does not lead to the hostility of dependence; opportunity for employment and, if necessary, supplemental income that does not require limiting active work; accessibility to existing devices allowing optimum use of residual hearing and vision and development of new aids for communication and mobility; and professionals trained to work with him and public agencies committed financially to providing for his special rehabilitation needs.

There are no easy answers to many of the problems of deaf-blindness. Its handicapping physical, psychological, and emotional implications, however, can be reduced if, as the deaf-blind person adjusts, society learns to accommodate.

Appendix A

Interview Questions in English

I. Past
  A. Geographical
    1. Where were you born? When?
    2. Did you grow up there? Where did you grow up?
    3. What sort of place was (*from above*)... large city, small town, rural area?
    4. What was your neighborhood like?
  B. Family
    1. Had your family lived in _____ for a long time?
    2. Did you have any brothers or sisters? How many? Are they older or younger than you?
    3. What did your parents do for work?
    4. What kind of upbringing did you have? For example, was it strict? Was your relationship with your parents close or distant?
    5. Did you have many relatives—aunts, uncles, cousins?
    6. How much contact did you have with them?
    7. Did you have close relationships with them?
  C. Growing Up (Educational, Social, Extracurricular Background by Age Groups)
    (ages 0-4)
      1. When did your parents find out you were blind?

2. How did they find out?
3. When did you start school? Was it a regular school or a special school? Did you have special classes?
4. What do you remember about that early schooling? Did you enjoy school? Were you bored?
5. Did you have any friends? Who were your friends?
6. What else do you remember from that period?

(ages 5-10, 12)
1. What do you remember about elementary school?
2. What were your teachers like?
3. Were you a serious student or did you fool around a lot?
4. What was your favorite subject?
5. Did you have many friends or not?
6. Who was your best friend?
7. What did you do in your spare time... for example, play baseball, play with dolls, read, listen to the radio?
8. Can you remember any story about when you were young... a particular time you remember?
9. What did you look like as a child?

(ages 12-15, 16)
1. Think about when you were older, in junior high school, what do you remember about school?
2. Were you studious or did you fool around a lot?
3. Did you get good grades in school?
4. What subject did you like best?
5. Did you have many friends?
6. What did you do in your spare time... after school and on weekends?
7. What did you do during the summers?

(ages 16 to end of high school)
1. When you were older, in high school, did you study hard?
2. Did you get good grades?
3. What was your favorite subject?
4. How would you rate your teachers?
5. Was there someone you really looked up to ... either someone you knew personally or someone famous?
6. What about friends... did you have many friends

or a few friends...?
7. Did you have any close friends?
8. Who was your best friend?
9. Were you a leader... for example, president of a club or captain of a team?
10. What did you do in your spare time... did you go out with boys/girls, play sports, read a lot, stay home and watch TV?

(after high school)
1. What did you do after high school?
2. (if school, ask general school questions again)
3. What do you remember from that period... were you generally satisfied and happy or not?
4. What did you do with your spare time?
5. How many different jobs have you had? What were the jobs?
6. Do you have a job now? How long have you been working at that job? How did you find that job?
7. What did you do for your first job? How did you find that one?

II. Present
A. Family
1. Are your parents living now? How often do you see your parents, brothers, sisters now?
2. How do you feel about your relationships with your parents, brothers, sisters?
3. Are you married?
4. When were you married? How did you meet your husband/wife?
5. Do you want to get married? Why?
6. Do you have any children? How many? How old are they?

B. Neighborhood
1. What kind of building do you live in... house, apartment...?
2. What sort of neighborhood is it? For example, do you feel safe there?

C. Work
1. Do you have a job now?
2. Are you satisfied with your job?

      3. What do you like/dislike about your job?
      4. Can you describe a typical day in your life?
- D. Social
  1. Do you have a hobby? What do you do at night, on weekends?
  2. Do you have any special talents, for example, in art, mechanics, cooking?
  3. Do you belong to any clubs or organizations?
  4. How much of your time do you spend with other people ... for example, are you with others most of the time, some of the time, never?
  5. Who are your friends ... people from work, from clubs, neighbors?
  6. What is your religion?
  7. Do you go to church regularly? Do you consider yourself religious?
  8. What are your best qualities ... for example, what are the things that make you good at your job, a good parent?
  9. What are your weaknesses and bad qualities?
- E. Other Questions
  1. When you look back and think about your past, what do you remember most strongly? What has made a real impression on your life?
  2. What is the most important thing in your life right now ... for example, your family, your work, your hobby?
  3. What do you think of the changes in the world that you see?
  4. Do you have any plans for the future ... for example, a goal to go to school or buy a house ... ?
  5. Do you ever think of changing parts of your life ... like where you live or your work ... what would you change?
  6. Is there anything that you really miss doing or seeing or hearing?
  7. How do you think that your life would be different if you were not deaf-blind ... do you think that you would do a different kind of work ... do a particular thing more often?
  8. As a deaf-blind person, do you have any particular

concerns about your future?
9. Do you think that sighted, hearing people have stereotypes about deaf-blind people? What are some stereotypes and myths that you think are wrong?
10. How do you feel about the services available to you as a deaf-blind person in your area and in the country?

Interview Questions in American Sign Language Format
I. Past
  A. Geographical
    1. When you born? Where?
    2. You grow-up (*name of place above*)? Where grow-up?
    3. Where you live (*name of place above*)... big city, small town, farm, o-r what?
    4. Near your home... people poor, rich, in-between o-r what?
  B. Family
    1. Your family... like grandmother, grandfather ... live (*name of place above*) before-before?
    2. You have brother, sister? How many? Older you...?
    3. Mother, father do-do-do work?
    4. Your mother, father... strict, easy... cooperate with you good, lousy, o-r what?
    5. Aunt, uncle, cousin... you have many-many aunts, uncles o-r few aunts, uncles?
    6. Aunts, uncles talk-talk-talk with you or little talk o-r no talk with you?
    7. Aunts, uncles close good to you... good, so-so, o-r lousy?
  C. Growing Up (Educational, Social, Extracurricular Background by Age Groups)
    (ages 0-4)
    1. When your mother, father find o-u-t you deaf, when?
    2. Find o-u-t how?
    3. When you start school? Hearing school... deaf school?

4. Enjoy school...bore school...what remember about school...like fight-fight-fight o-r what?
5. You small...born to 4...you have any friend? Your friends, who?
6. Remember other things?

(ages 5-10, 12)
1. You small boy/girl...5 to 10 years old...what remember about school?
2. Teachers good, so-so, lousy o-r what?
3. You study hard o-r play-play-play?
4. You like everything...what you like best ...math, English, o-r what?
5. Small...you have friends many-many or few?
6. Who your best friend...*friend*?
7. You small play baseball, play d-o-l-l-s, read-read-read, watch T-V o-r what?
8. Can you tell me story about you small...fun time, so-so time, lousy time...what-what-what?
9. You see pictures you small boy/girl...now still remember same pictures *now*?

(ages 12-15, 16)
1. You grow-up...now j-r h-s...what remember about school?
2. You study hard or play-play-play?
3. You get good g-r-a-d-e-s?
4. What you like best...math, English...what?
5. Have friends many-many o-r few?
6. Do-do-do Saturday, Sunday, after school...play baseball, read-read, stay home watch T/V, o-r what?
7. Do-do-do summer?

(ages 16 to end of high school)
1. You older...h-s...h-s you study hard or play-play-play?
2. Get good g-r-a-d-e-s?
3. What you like best...math, English o-r what?
4. Teachers good, so-so, o-r lousy?
5. Look-back years before, look u-p someone you like...teacher, famous person...who?
6. Have friends many-many o-r few?
7. Close friends *friend*?
8. Your best friend who?

9. You leader ... president your class, c-l-u-b-s, captain football team?
10. You teenager do-do-do ... go-out girls/boys ... play football, baseball ... read-read-read ... stay home watch T-V o-r what?

(after high school)
1. Finish h-s when what year? ... First j-o-b start when what year? Do-do-do 19____ ... 19____ between?
2. (if school, ask general school questions again)
3. Remember about (*from above*) still remember what-what- ... like many many good times ... so-so times, lousy times o-r what?
4. Do-do-do ... go-out again-again-again ... stay home ... work hard ...?
5. How-many different different j-o-b-s before? What-what-what j-o-b-s?
6. Have j-o-b now? How long you work that j-o-b? (#) years ago ... how you find j-o-b?
7. Do-do your first j-o-b? How you find that j-o-b?

II. Present
A. Family
1. Your mother, father live now? How many times you see-see your mother, father, sister, brother in 1976, 1977?
2. You feel good o-r bad to see your mother, father, sister, brother?
3. You married?
4. Marry when? How meet husband/wife?
5. You want marry? Why?
6. Have children? How many? How old?

B. Neighborhood
1. You live in house, a-p-t o-r what?
2. You feel safe walk out your home?

C. Work
1. You have j-o-b now?
2. Satisfied with j-o-b?
3. Why you like/don't like j-o-b?
4. Do-do-do every-day? What you do every-morning, every afternoon?

D. Social
   1. What your h-o-b-b-y? What do-do every-night, Saturday, Sunday?
   2. You good skill with draw, cook, mechanics, o-r what?
   3. Belong any group... like deaf c-l-u-b, bowl c-l-u-b?
   4. You with many people every-day o-r many people sometimes o-r alone every-day?
   5. You many friends o-r few friends nights, weekend?
   6. Your friends... who? Live near your home? From work? From deaf c-l-u-b?
   7. What your religion?
   8. Go church every Sunday? You read Bible, think about God... every-day... sometimes... never o-r what?
   9. What good things about you make you good at j-o-b o-r make you good mother/father?
   10. What lousy things about you what bad habit ... like some people say... know me lazy, me not patient enough...?

E. Other Questions
   1. Look-back... years-years before-before... think ... about what most important... you never forget?
   2. What now *now* most important in your life... work o-r family o-r h-o-b-b-y o-r what?
   3. World change from before... now more-more-more change... you like that... why?
   4. Plan-plan for future? What plan... have goal like go school... buy house... what plan?
   5. You think about move new home... change j-o-b ... what you like... *wish* change-change?
   6. Before... you see... look-around... but now can't see, can't hear... you miss? Movies, driving, what...?
   7. You suppose you not deaf-blind, what you want work... where live... what else you want?
   8. Now you can't see, can't hear... you worry about future... what worry?
   9. Group deaf-blind... group hearing... hearing look-at deaf-blind... hearing think deaf-blind

stupid o-r same-same ... o-r different o-r what ... what hearing think?
10. Home house area ... interpreter helps you, doctor helps you, lawyer helps you ... how? You like _____ help? You want _____ help? Why you like/want?

Appendix B

The two authorization forms that follow were produced in standard sized print, large print, and Braille as necessary. When appropriate, sign language interpreters interpreted the contents of the authorizations to deaf-blind individuals. In those instances, the Interpreter's Statement of Acknowledgment was included and signed on the authorization forms.

Appendix B

AUTHORIZATION STATEMENT

Public Service Programs of Gallaudet College is undertaking a project to interview deaf-blind individuals and then write and publish a collection of biographies based on those interviews. The kind of information asked in each set of interviews will concern an individual's development from childhood to adulthood, covering family life, schooling, work, social life, and thoughts and feelings related to being deaf-blind. The purpose of the collection is to provide accurate information on the personal, everyday aspects of deaf-blindness for professional workers in education, health, and social services. Gallaudet does not want to cause embarrassment to an individual, and will therefore use pseudonyms and change the names of locations in the biographies, either at the request of the deaf-blind person, or when the College considers it advisable. At the same time, the College believes it is crucial to give an accurate description of the life of the individual, based on the information the person relays and the impressions of the interviewer. The contents of the written biography will be communicated back to the individual before it is published to check the accuracy of the factual information. Changes in the manuscript may be made at that time to insure accuracy of the biographical information previously relayed.

Please check yes or no for each of the following 3 statements.

Yes No

___ ___ I would like a pseudonym used instead of my name.

___ ___ I would like the names of locations changed.

___ ___ I authorize Gallaudet College to decide to use a pseudonym and/or change the names of locations.

I have read and understand the preceding paragraph and I authorize Gallaudet College to publish a biography of my life, based on interviews, in accordance with the purpose and methods described above. I transfer to Gallaudet College any and all literary rights I might have in the published book.

Signature _____

Witness _____

Date _____

AUTHORIZATION STATEMENT

I give permission for Carol Yoken of Public Service Programs, Gallaudet College and/or _____

to contact people who have known me (both in the past and presently)–including parents, siblings, other relatives, teachers, social service workers and others–who can supply information about my life. The above-named persons have my permission to consult with the other people both before and after Carol Yoken interviews me, in order for her to get a fuller picture of my life and to confirm information that I give in the interviews.

Signature _____

Witness _____

Date _____

INTERPRETER'S STATEMENT OF ACKNOWLEDGMENT

I hereby certify that I am a qualified interpreter for deaf and deaf-blind persons, and that I am able to communicate freely with _____ , who is deaf and
          (name of interviewee)
blind. The explanations referred to in the foregoing authorization were made through me to _____
                                       (name of interviewee)
in a language which he/she understood.

Signature _____

Date _____

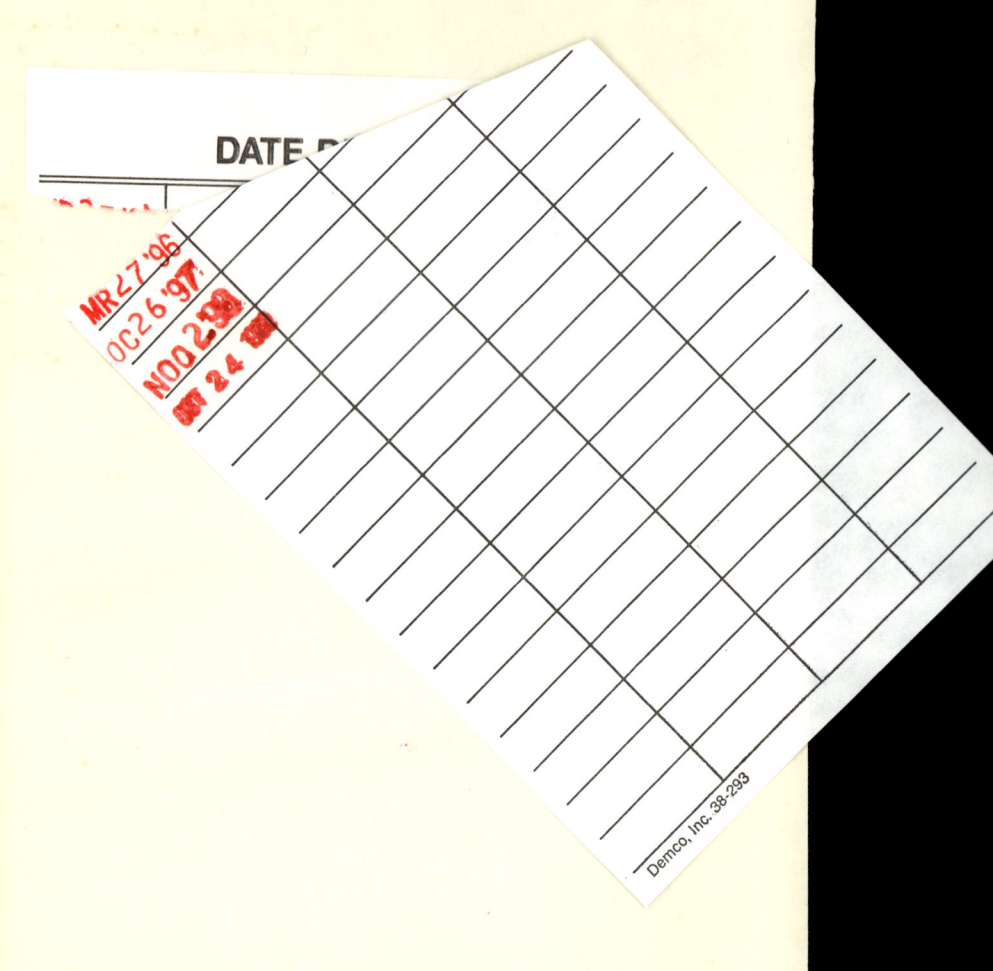